Take It to Your Seat Centers
Common Core Language K

Common Core Language Standard CCLS	Center	Skill	Page
CCLS K.1b	Nouns	Use nouns in sentences	7
CCLS K.1b	Action Verbs	Use verbs in sentences	19
CCLS K.1c	Plural Nouns	Use plural nouns	31
CCLS K.1d	Question Words	Use question words in sentences	43
CCLS K.1e	Prepositions	Show meaning of prepositions in sentences; choose correct prepositions	59
CCLS K.2a	Capital Letters	Use capital letters for the beginning of sentences and for the pronoun *I*	71
CCLS K.2b	End Punctuation	Sort and match end punctuation to show meaning	83
CCLS K.2c, K.2d	Spell Words	Use letters and sounds to form words	95
CCLS K.4	Multiple-Meaning Words	Match multiple-meaning words with the correct pictures	109
CCLS K.4b	Inflections and Affixes	Match words with inflections and affixes to root words	123
CCLS K.5a	Sorting	Sort objects and name the groups	137
CCLS K.5b	Opposites	Match opposites to show understanding of word meaning	149

© Evan-Moor Corp. • EMC 2870 • Take It to Your Seat Centers—Language

Using the Centers

The 12 centers in this book provide hands-on practice to help students master standards-based language skills. It is important to teach each skill and to model the use of each center before asking students to do the tasks independently. The centers are self-contained and portable. Students can work at a desk, at a table, or on a rug, and they can use the centers as often as needed.

Why Use Centers?

- Centers are a motivating way for students to practice important skills.
- They provide for differentiated instruction.
- They support kinesthetic and visual learners.
- They can be used for teaching skills or for informal assessments.

Before Using the Centers

Here are a few things to consider:

- Will students select a center, or will you assign the centers and use them as a skill assessment tool?
- Will there be a specific block of time for centers, or will the centers be used by students throughout the day as they complete other work?
- What procedure will students use when they need help with the center tasks?
- Will students use the answer key to check their own work?

Introducing the Centers

Use the teacher instructions page and the student directions on the center's cover page to teach or review the skill. Show students the center and model how to use it as you read each step of the directions.

Recording Progress

Reproduce the Center Checklist (page 4) and use it to record the date when a student completes each center and the student's skill level.

I Can Statements

Reproduce enough *I Can* statements to give one of each to each student. Then cut apart the statements, and choose one of the options below:

Option 1: Put each statement with its corresponding center and instruct students to take one upon completion of each center.

Option 2: Distribute each statement to students after you correct and return their written practice page.

You may wish to have students display the *I Can* statements on a bulletin board, in a learning log, or in their student portfolios.

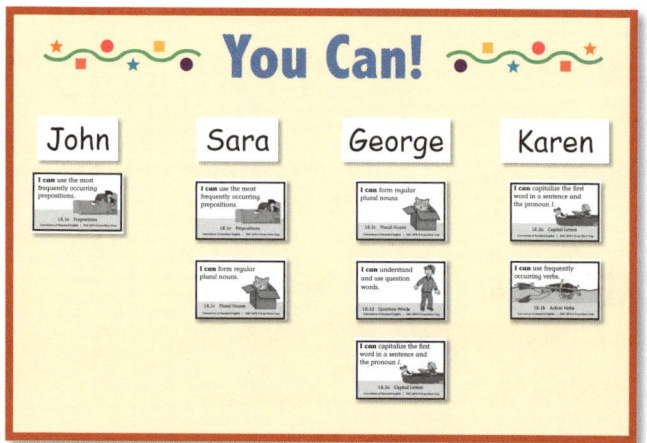

Making the Centers

Included for Each Center
- **A** Student directions/cover page
- **B** Mats and task cards
- **C** Reproducible activity
- **D** Answer key

Materials Needed
- Folders with inside pockets
- Small envelopes or self-closing plastic bags (for storing task cards)
- Pencils or marking pens (for labeling envelopes)
- Scissors
- Double-sided tape, glue stick, or stapler (for attaching the cover page to the front of the folder)
- Laminating equipment

How to Assemble and Store
1. Attach the center's cover page to the front of the folder.
2. Place reproduced activity pages in the left-hand pocket of the folder.
3. Cut apart the task cards. Then laminate the mats and task cards.
4. Cut apart the laminated task cards and put them in a labeled envelope or self-closing plastic bag. Place the mats and task cards in the right-hand pocket of the folder. If you want the centers to be self-checking, include the answer key in the folder.
5. Store prepared centers in a file box or a crate.

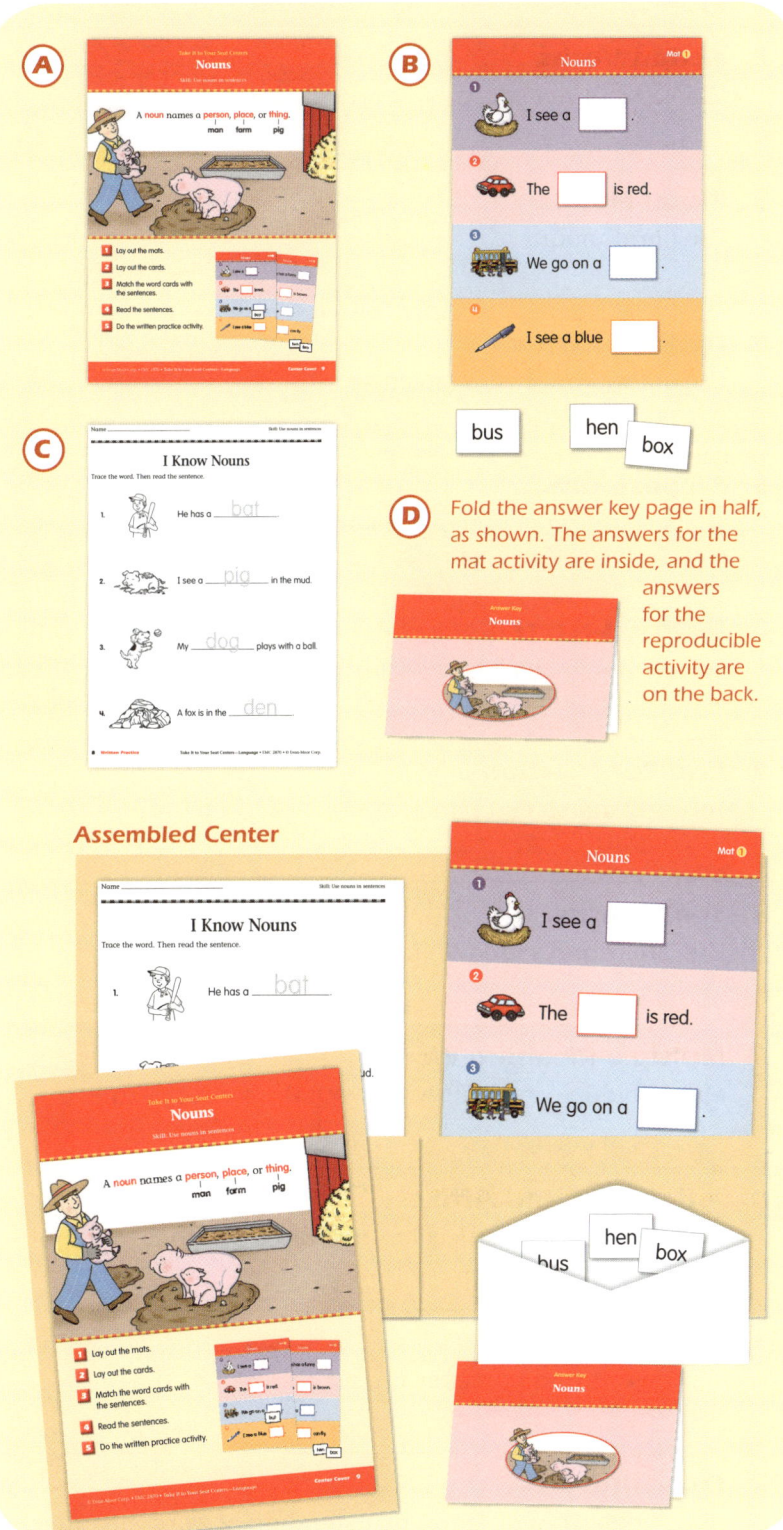

© Evan-Moor Corp. • EMC 2870 • *Take It to Your Seat Centers—Language*

Student _____

Note: Reproduce and record student progress.

Center Checklist

Center / Skill	Skill Level	Date
1. Nouns Use nouns in sentences		
2. Action Verbs Use verbs in sentences		
3. Plural Nouns Use plural nouns		
4. Question Words Use question words in sentences		
5. Prepositions Show meaning of prepositions in sentences; choose correct prepositions		
6. Capital Letters Use capital letters for the beginning of sentences and for the pronoun *I*		
7. End Punctuation Sort and match end punctuation to show meaning		
8. Spell Words Use letters and sounds to form words		
9. Multiple-Meaning Words Match multiple-meaning words with the correct pictures		
10. Inflections and Affixes Match words with inflections and affixes to root words		
11. Sorting Sort objects and name the groups		
12. Opposites Match opposites to show understanding of word meaning		

Take It to Your Seat Centers—Language • EMC 2870 • © Evan-Moor Corp.

I Can Statements

Note: Reproduce for each student.

I can use nouns.

LK.1b   Nouns
Conventions of Standard English | EMC 2870 © Evan-Moor Corp.

I can use verbs.

LK.1b   Action Verbs
Conventions of Standard English | EMC 2870 © Evan-Moor Corp.

I can form regular plural nouns.

LK.1c   Plural Nouns
Conventions of Standard English | EMC 2870 © Evan-Moor Corp.

I can use question words.

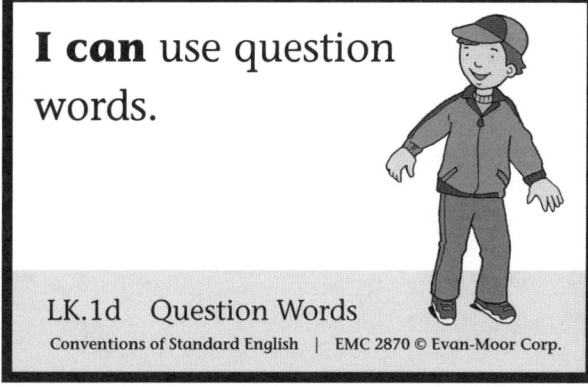

LK.1d   Question Words
Conventions of Standard English | EMC 2870 © Evan-Moor Corp.

I can use prepositions.

LK.1e   Prepositions
Conventions of Standard English | EMC 2870 © Evan-Moor Corp.

I can capitalize the first word in a sentence and the pronoun *I*.

LK.2a   Capital Letters
Conventions of Standard English | EMC 2870 © Evan-Moor Corp.

I Can Statements

Note: Reproduce for each student.

I can name end punctuation.

LK.2b   End Punctuation
Conventions of Standard English | EMC 2870 © Evan-Moor Corp.

I can write the letters for consonants and short-vowel sounds.

LK.2c, LK.2d   Spell Words
Conventions of Standard English | EMC 2870 © Evan-Moor Corp.

I can understand multiple-meaning words and phrases.

LK.4   Multiple-Meaning Words
Vocabulary Acquisition and Use | EMC 2870 © Evan-Moor Corp.

I can use inflections and affixes.

LK.4b   Inflections and Affixes
Vocabulary Acquisition and Use | EMC 2870 © Evan-Moor Corp.

I can sort objects into categories.
LK.5a   Sorting
Vocabulary Acquisition and Use | EMC 2870 © Evan-Moor Corp.

I can understand verbs and adjectives and their opposites.
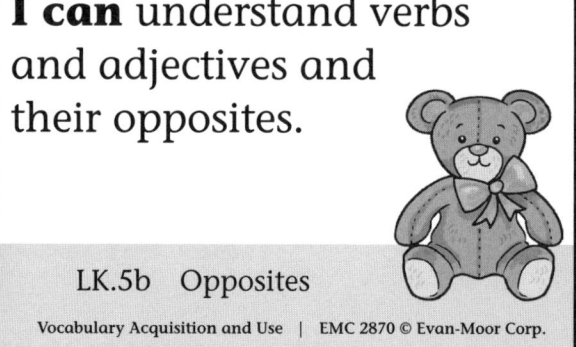
LK.5b   Opposites
Vocabulary Acquisition and Use | EMC 2870 © Evan-Moor Corp.

Take It to Your Seat Centers

Nouns

Center Cover

Answer Key

Written Practice

Mats

Cards

CCLS K.1b Use frequently occurring nouns and verbs

Skill: Use nouns in sentences

Steps to Follow

1. **Prepare the center.** (See page 3.)
2. **Introduce the center.** State the goal. Say: *You will use nouns to complete sentences.*
3. **Teach the skill.** Demonstrate how to use the center.
4. **Practice the skill.** Have students complete the center tasks independently or with a partner.

Contents

Written Practice..... 8
Center Cover.......... 9
Answer Key............ 11
Center Mats........... 13
Cards 17

Name _____

Skill: Use nouns in sentences

I Know Nouns

Trace the word. Then read the sentence.

1.  He has a ___bat___.

2.  I see a ___pig___ in the mud.

3.  My ___dog___ plays with a ball.

4.  A fox is in the ___den___.

8 Written Practice

Take It to Your Seat Centers—Language • EMC 2870 • © Evan-Moor Corp.

Take It to Your Seat Centers

Nouns

Skill: Use nouns in sentences

A **noun** names a **person**, **place**, or **thing**.
man   farm   pig

1 Lay out the mats.

2 Lay out the cards.

3 Match the word cards with the sentences.

4 Read the sentences.

5 Do the written practice activity.

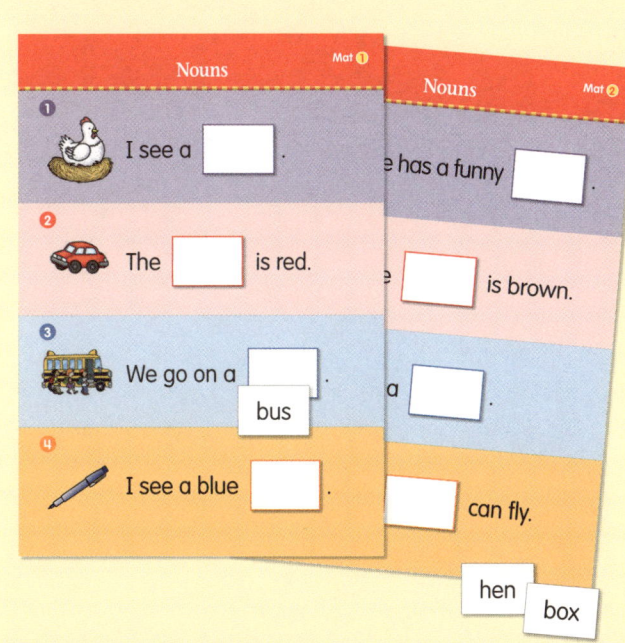

© Evan-Moor Corp. • EMC 2870 • Take It to Your Seat Centers—Language

Center Cover 9

Written Practice

I Know Nouns

Name _____

Skill: Use nouns in sentences

Trace the word. Then read the sentence.

1. He has a **bat**.
2. I see a **pig** in the mud.
3. My **dog** plays with a ball.
4. A fox is in the **den**.

Nouns

Answer Key

Answer Key

Nouns

Mat 1

Nouns

1. I see a hen .
2. The car is red.
3. We go on a bus .
4. I see a blue pen .

Mat 2

Nouns

1. He has a funny hat .
2. The box is brown.
3. It is a cat .
4. The bee can fly.

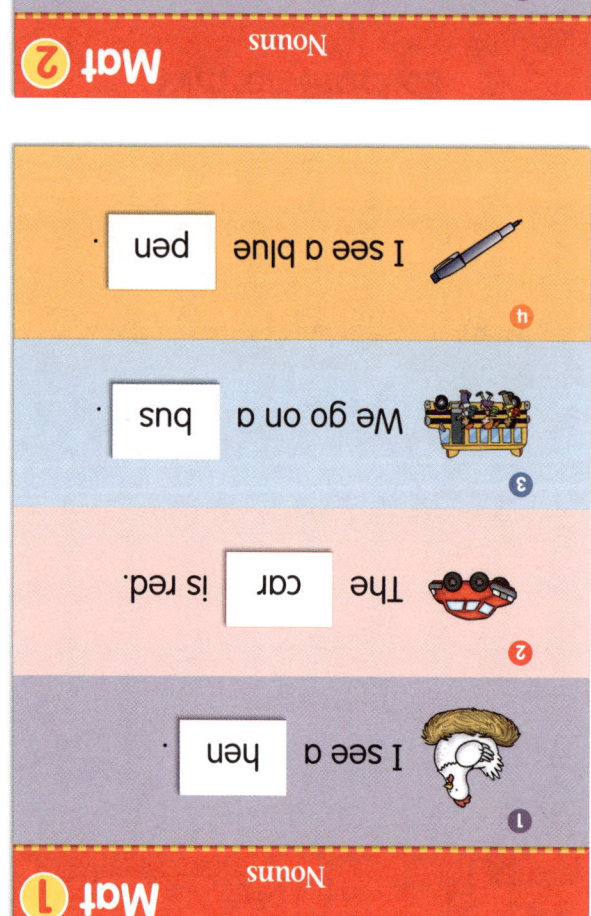

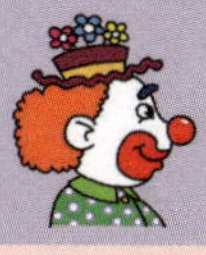

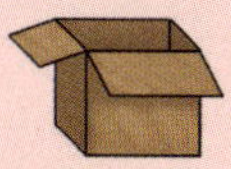

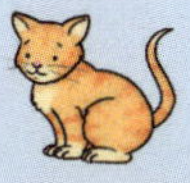

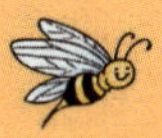

Nouns

Mat 1

1 
 I see a ☐ .

2
 The ☐ is red.

3
 We go on a ☐ .

4
 I see a blue ☐ .

14 Center Mat

Nouns

Mat 2

1

   He has a funny  .

2

   The  is brown.

3

   It is a  .

4

   The  can fly.

Cards for Mats 1 and 2

hen	hat
car	box
bus	cat
pen	bee

Nouns	**Nouns**
EMC 2870	EMC 2870
© Evan-Moor Corp.	© Evan-Moor Corp.

Nouns	**Nouns**
EMC 2870	EMC 2870
© Evan-Moor Corp.	© Evan-Moor Corp.

Nouns	**Nouns**
EMC 2870	EMC 2870
© Evan-Moor Corp.	© Evan-Moor Corp.

Nouns	**Nouns**
EMC 2870	EMC 2870
© Evan-Moor Corp.	© Evan-Moor Corp.

Take It to Your Seat Centers

Action Verbs

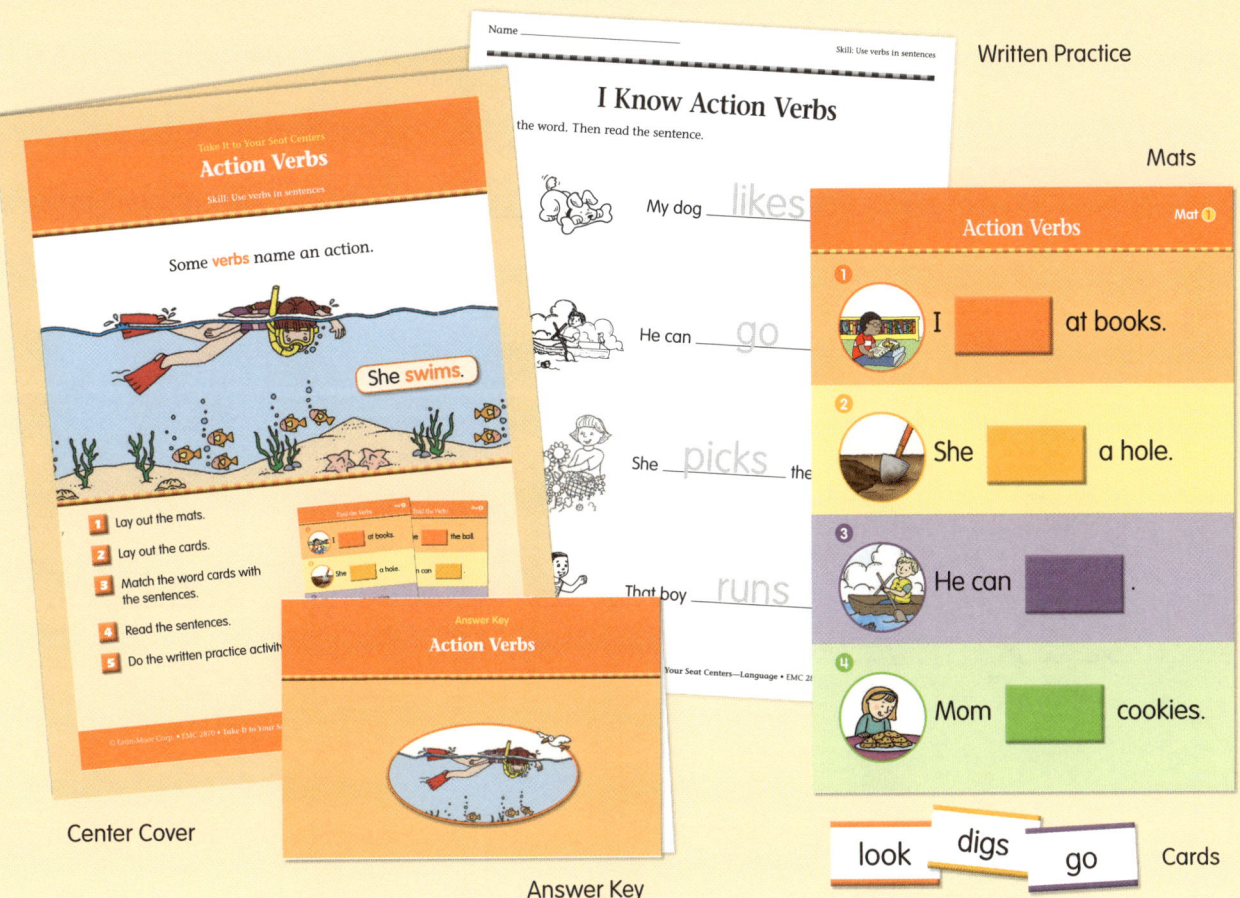

CCLS **K.1b** Use frequently occurring nouns and verbs

Skill: Use verbs in sentences

Steps to Follow

1. **Prepare the center.** (See page 3.)
2. **Introduce the center.** State the goal. Say: *You will use verbs to complete sentences.*
3. **Teach the skill.** Demonstrate how to use the center.
4. **Practice the skill.** Have students complete the center tasks independently or with a partner.

Contents

Written Practice..... 20

Center Cover 21

Answer Key 23

Center Mats 25

Cards 29

Name _____   Skill: Use verbs in sentences

I Know Action Verbs

Trace the word. Then read the sentence.

1.  My dog ___likes___ the bone.

2.  He can ___go___ in a boat.

3.  She ___picks___ the flowers.

4.  That boy ___runs___ fast.

Take It to Your Seat Centers

Action Verbs

Skill: Use verbs in sentences

Some **verbs** name an action.

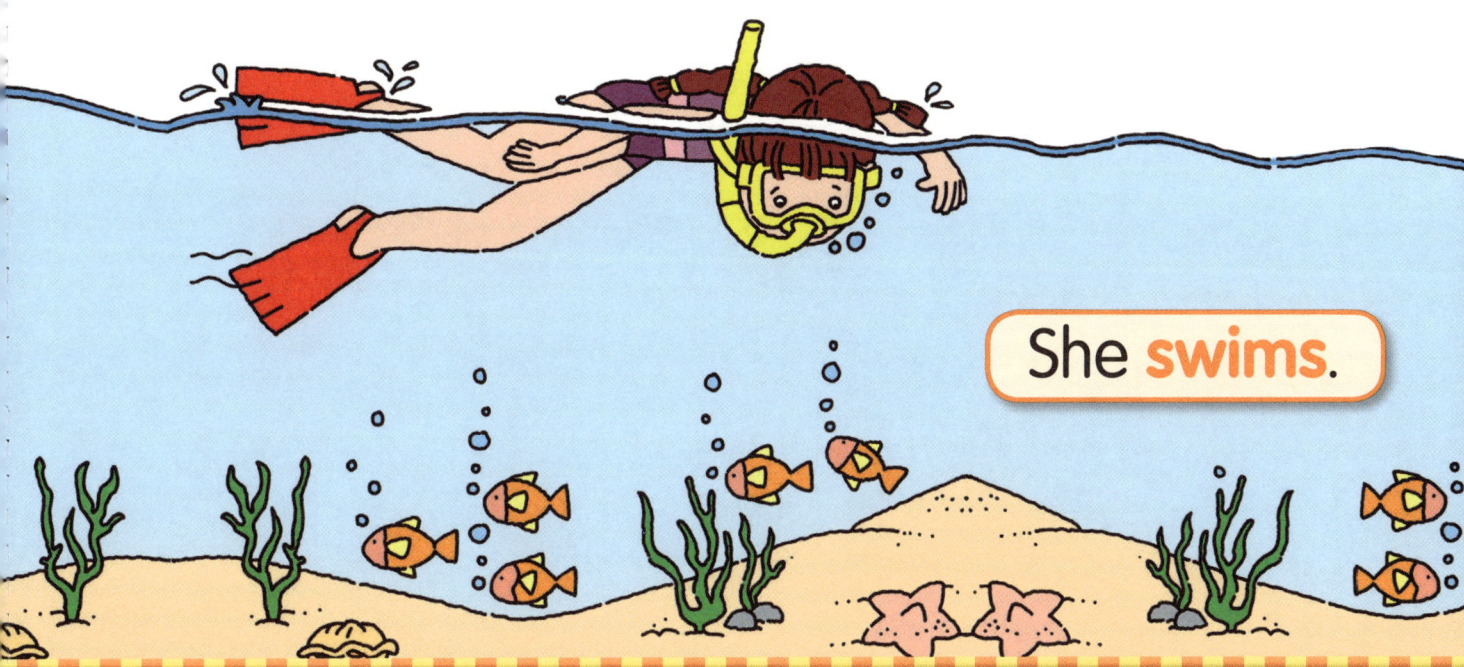

She **swims**.

1. Lay out the mats.
2. Lay out the cards.
3. Match the word cards with the sentences.
4. Read the sentences.
5. Do the written practice activity.

Written Practice

I Know Action Verbs

Trace the word. Then read the sentence.

1. My dog **likes** the bone.
2. He can **go** in a boat.
3. She **picks** the flowers.
4. That boy **runs** fast.

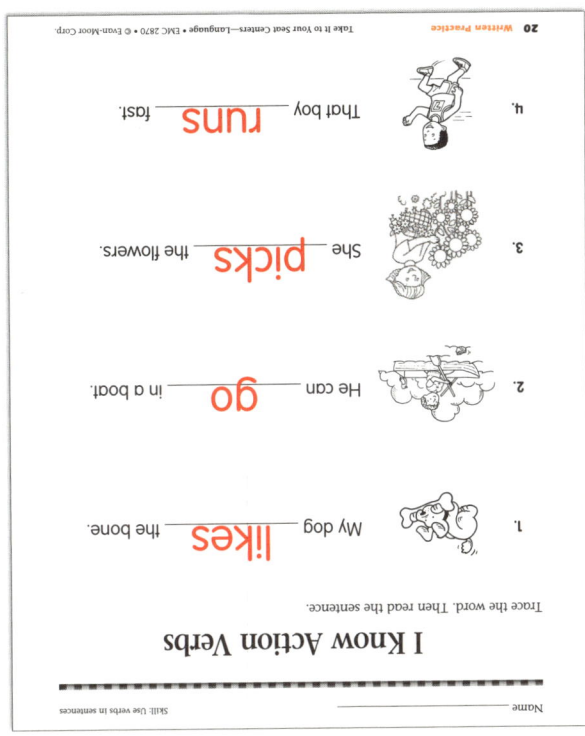

Answer Key

Action Verbs

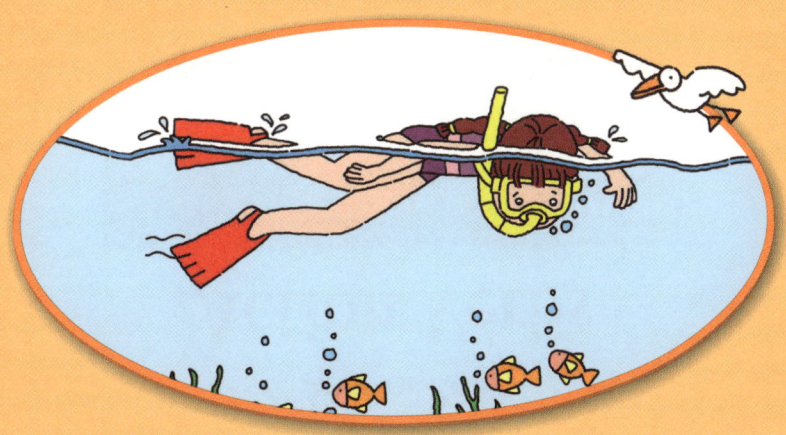

Answer Key
Action Verbs

Mat 1 — Action Verbs
1. I **look** at books.
2. She **digs** a hole.
3. He can **go**.
4. Mom **makes** cookies.

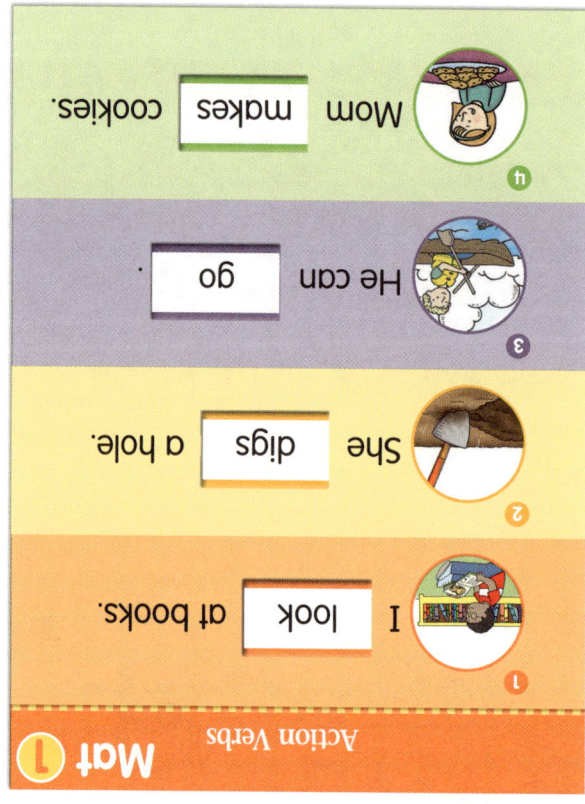

Mat 2 — Action Verbs
1. She **hits** the ball.
2. Dan can **run**.
3. Ben **plays** all day.
4. The hen **sits**.

Action Verbs

Mat 1

1 I ____ at books.

2 She ____ a hole.

3 He can ____ .

4 Mom ____ cookies.

Action Verbs

Mat 2

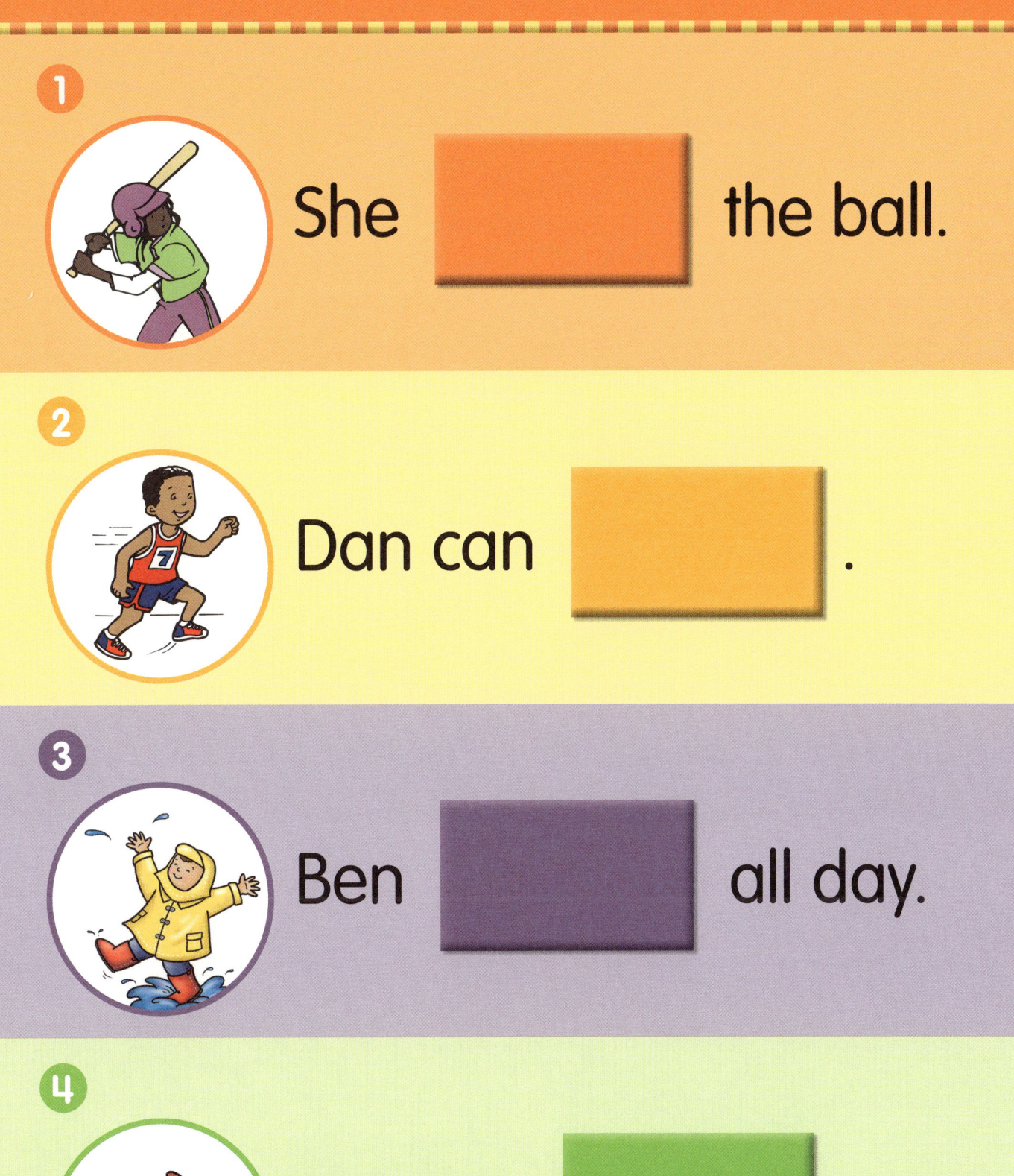

Cards for Mats 1 and 2

look	hits
digs	run
go	plays
makes	sits

Action Verbs EMC 2870 © Evan-Moor Corp.	**Action Verbs** EMC 2870 © Evan-Moor Corp.
Action Verbs EMC 2870 © Evan-Moor Corp.	**Action Verbs** EMC 2870 © Evan-Moor Corp.
Action Verbs EMC 2870 © Evan-Moor Corp.	**Action Verbs** EMC 2870 © Evan-Moor Corp.
Action Verbs EMC 2870 © Evan-Moor Corp.	**Action Verbs** EMC 2870 © Evan-Moor Corp.

Take It to Your Seat Centers
Plural Nouns

CCLS K.1c Form regular plural nouns orally by adding /s/ or /es/

Skill: Use plural nouns

Steps to Follow

1. **Prepare the center.** (See page 3.)

2. **Introduce the center.** State the goal. Say: *You will match plural nouns to pictures.*

3. **Teach the skill.** Demonstrate how to use the center.

4. **Practice the skill.** Have students complete the center tasks independently or with a partner.

Contents

Written Practice..... 32

Center Cover.......... 33

Answer Key............ 35

Center Mats........... 37

Cards 41

© Evan-Moor Corp. • EMC 2870 • Take It to Your Seat Centers—Language   Teacher Instructions **31**

Name _____   Skill: Use plural nouns

I Know Plural Nouns

Trace the word. Read the words.

1.

   pan   pans

2.

   bug   bugs

3.

   fox   foxes

32 Written Practice   Take It to Your Seat Centers—Language • EMC 2870 • © Evan-Moor Corp.

Take It to Your Seat Centers

Plural Nouns

Skill: Use plural nouns

Add -s or -es to make a plural noun.

1. Lay out the mats.
2. Lay out the cards.
3. Match the word cards with the pictures.
4. Read the words.
5. Do the written practice activity.

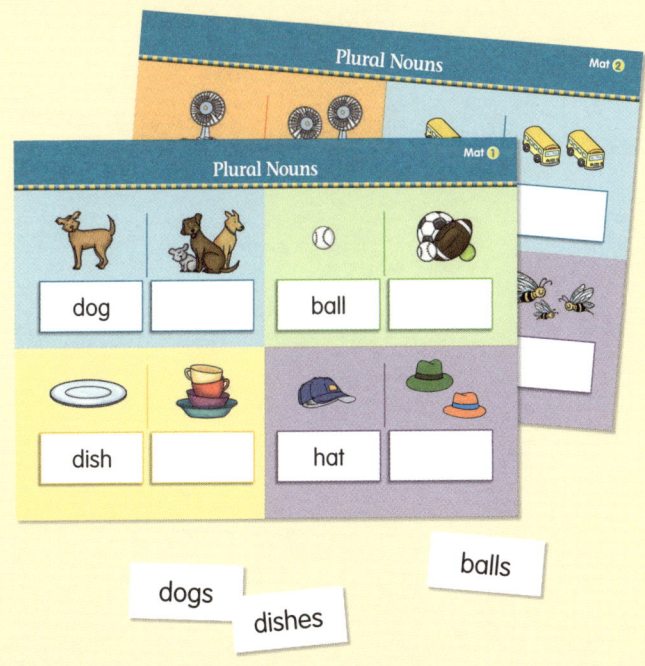

Written Practice

I Know Plural Nouns

Trace the word. Read the words.

1. pan — pans
2. bug — bugs
3. fox — foxes

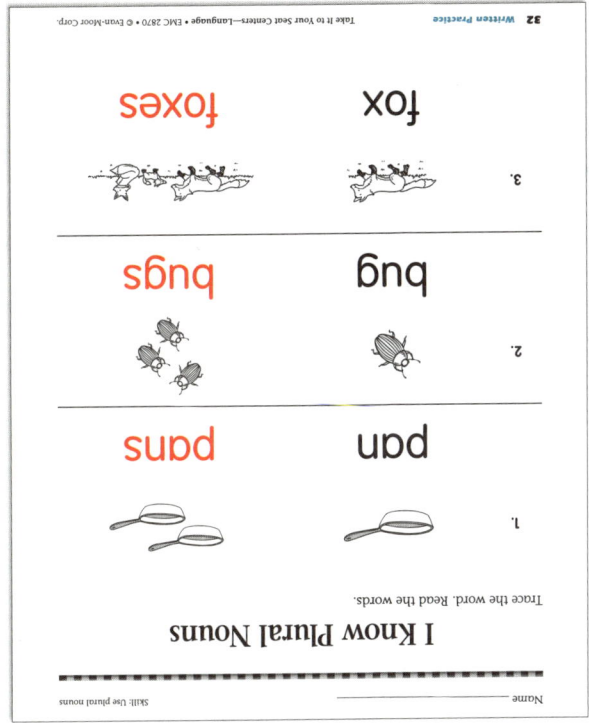

Plural Nouns

Answer Key

Answer Key
Plural Nouns

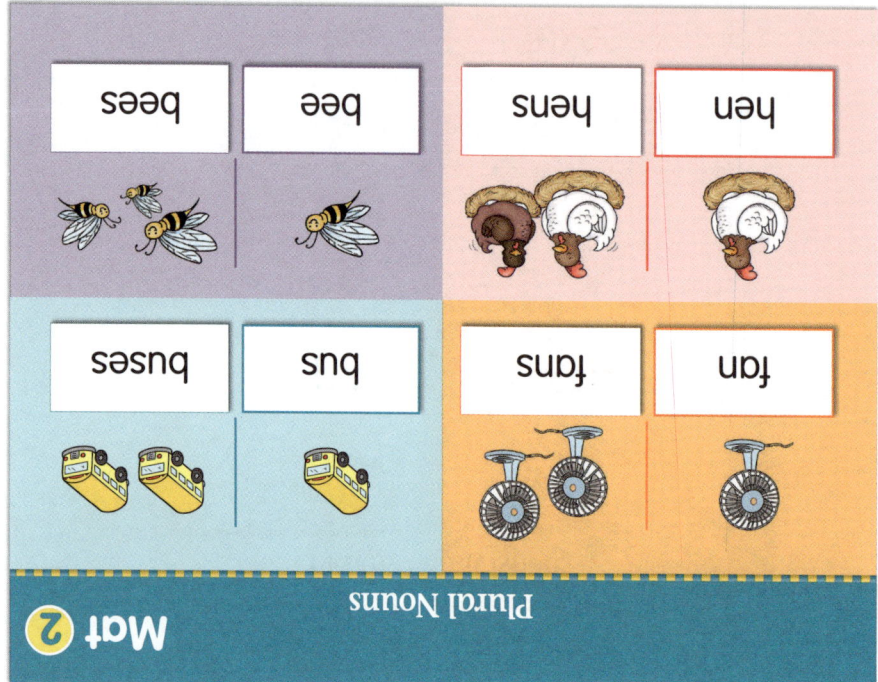

Plural Nouns

Mat 1

ball

hat

dog

dish

Plural Nouns

Mat 2

bus

bee

fan

hen

Cards for Mats 1 and 2

dogs	fans
balls	buses
dishes	hens
hats	bees

Plural Nouns
EMC 2870
© Evan-Moor Corp.

Plural Nouns
EMC 2870
© Evan-Moor Corp.

Plural Nouns
EMC 2870
© Evan-Moor Corp.

Plural Nouns
EMC 2870
© Evan-Moor Corp.

Plural Nouns
EMC 2870
© Evan-Moor Corp.

Plural Nouns
EMC 2870
© Evan-Moor Corp.

Plural Nouns
EMC 2870
© Evan-Moor Corp.

Plural Nouns
EMC 2870
© Evan-Moor Corp.

Take It to Your Seat Centers

Question Words

Written Practice

Mats

Center Cover

Answer Key

Cards

CCLS K.1d Understand and use question words

Skill: Use question words in sentences

Steps to Follow

1. **Prepare the center.** (See page 3.)
2. **Introduce the center.** State the goal. Say: *You will use question words in sentences.*
3. **Teach the skill.** Demonstrate how to use the center.
4. **Practice the skill.** Have students complete the center tasks independently or with a partner.

Contents

Written Practice..... 44

Center Cover.......... 45

Answer Key............ 47

Center Mats........... 49

Cards 55

© Evan-Moor Corp. • EMC 2870 • Take It to Your Seat Centers—Language

Teacher Instructions 43

Name _____

Skill: Use question words in sentences

I Know Question Words

Draw a line to match.

1. **Who** is wet?

He is wet.

2. **Where** is he?

He can jump.

3. **How** can he get out?

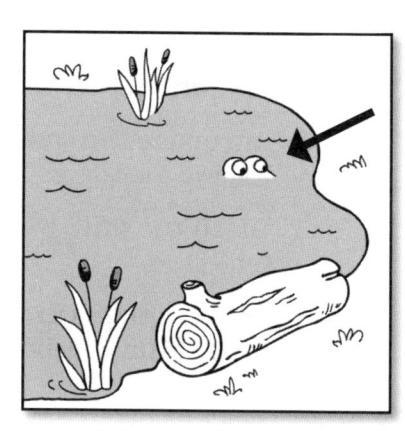

He is here.

Take It to Your Seat Centers

Question Words

Skill: Use question words in sentences

Some words help you ask a **question**.

Who will you see?

Where are you going?

How will you go?

1. Lay out the mats.
2. Put the cards in sets by color.
3. Put each set with its mat.
4. Match the question sentence with the answer sentence.
5. Do the written practice activity.

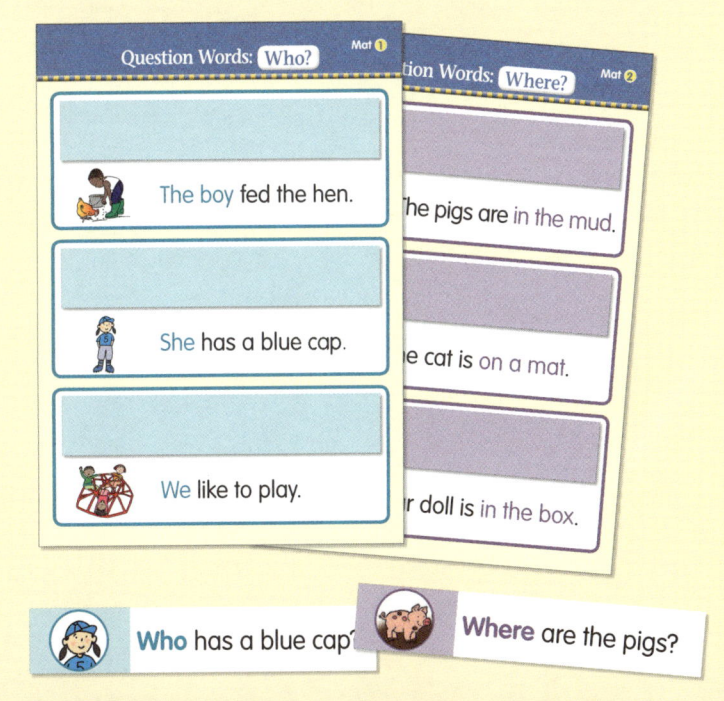

Question Words: Who? Mat 1
The boy fed the hen.
She has a blue cap.
We like to play.

Question Words: Where? Mat 2
The pigs are in the mud.
The cat is on a mat.
The doll is in the box.

Who has a blue cap? Where are the pigs?

© Evan-Moor Corp. • EMC 2870 • Take It to Your Seat Centers—Language   Center Cover 45

Answer Key

Question Words

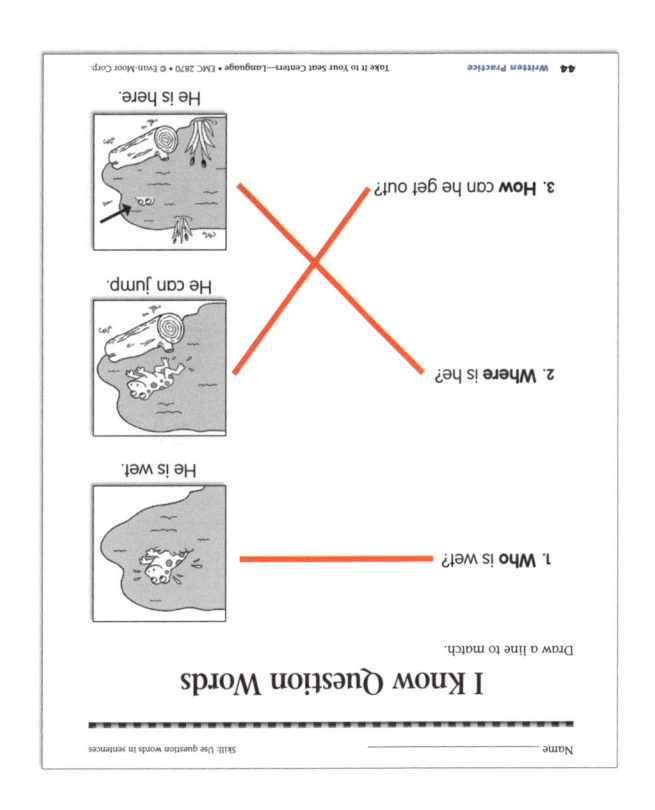

Written Practice

I Know Question Words

Draw a line to match.

1. **Who** is wet? — He is wet.
2. **Where** is he? — He can jump.
3. **How** can he get out? — He is here.

Answer Key

Question Words

Mat 1 — Question Words: **Who?**

- **Who** fed the hen?
- The boy fed the hen.
- **Who** has a blue cap?
- She has a blue cap.
- **Who** likes to play?
- We like to play.

Mat 2 — Question Words: **Where?**

- **Where** are the pigs?
- The pigs are in the mud.
- **Where** is the cat?
- The cat is on a mat.
- **Where** is your doll?
- Your doll is in the box.

Mat 3 — Question Words: **How?**

- **How** can it get out?
- It can tap, tap, tap.
- **How** do you go?
- We go on the bus.
- **How** will you find me?
- Look and see!

Question Words: Who?

Mat 1

The boy fed the hen.

She has a blue cap.

We like to play.

Question Words: Where?

Mat 2

The pigs are in the mud.

The cat is on a mat.

Your doll is in the box.

Question Words: How?

Mat 3

It can tap, tap, tap.

We go on the bus.

Look and see!

Cards for Mats 1 and 2

Who fed the hen?

Who has a blue cap?

Who likes to play?

Where are the pigs?

Where is the cat?

Where is your doll?

Question Words

EMC 2870 • © Evan-Moor Corp.

Question Words

EMC 2870 • © Evan-Moor Corp.

Question Words

EMC 2870 • © Evan-Moor Corp.

Question Words

EMC 2870 • © Evan-Moor Corp.

Question Words

EMC 2870 • © Evan-Moor Corp.

Question Words

EMC 2870 • © Evan-Moor Corp.

Cards for Mat 3

How can it get out?

How do you go?

How will you find me?

Question Words

EMC 2870 • © Evan-Moor Corp.

Question Words

EMC 2870 • © Evan-Moor Corp.

Question Words

EMC 2870 • © Evan-Moor Corp.

Take It to Your Seat Centers

Prepositions

Written Practice

Mats

Center Cover

Answer Key

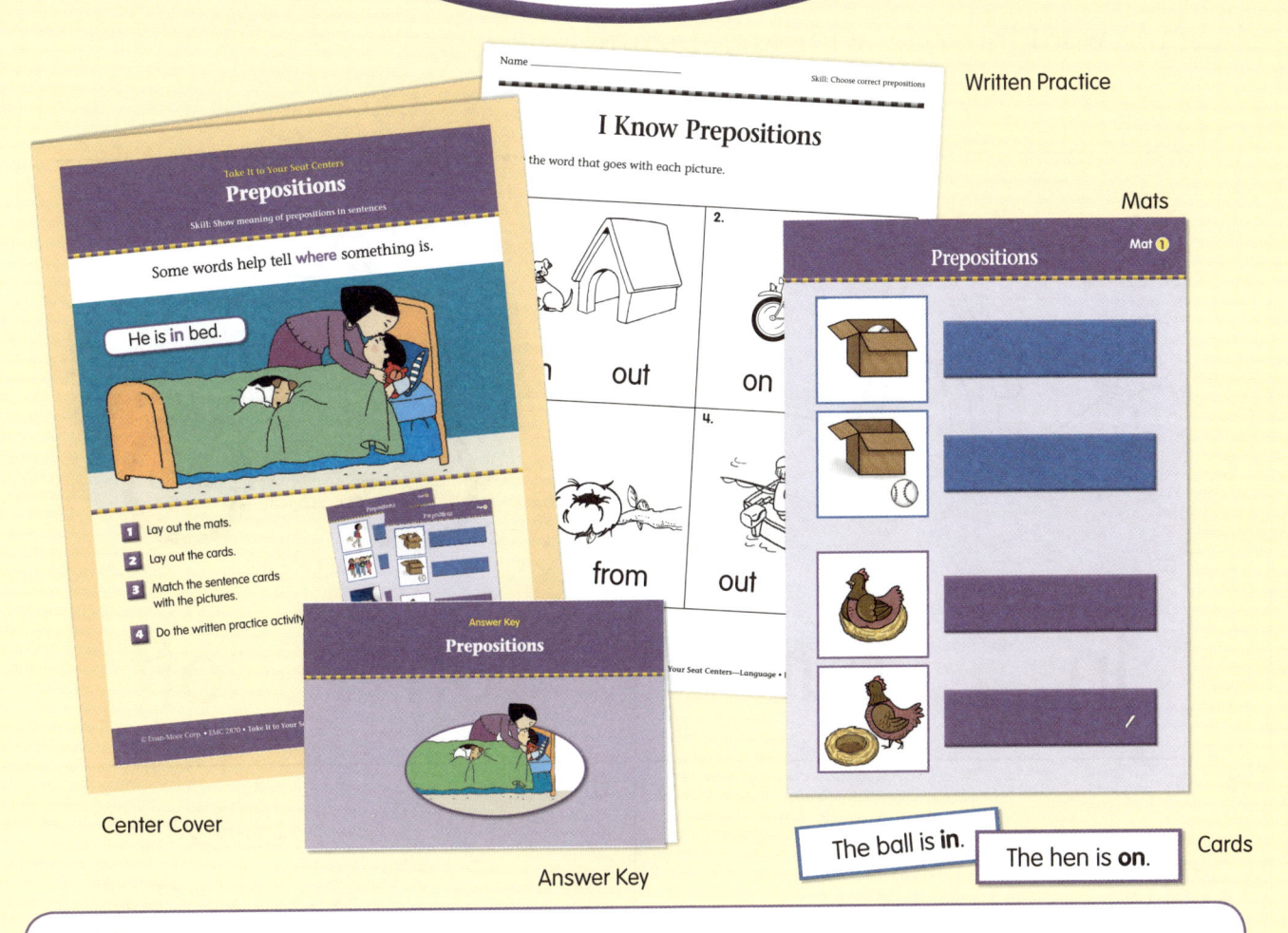

Cards

CCLS K.1e Use the most frequently occurring prepositions

Skill: Show meaning of prepositions in sentences; choose correct prepositions

Steps to Follow

1. **Prepare the center.** (See page 3.)
2. **Introduce the center.** State the goal. Say: *You will use prepositions in sentences.*
3. **Teach the skill.** Demonstrate how to use the center.
4. **Practice the skill.** Have students complete the center tasks independently or with a partner.

Contents

Written Practice..... 60

Center Cover.......... 61

Answer Key............ 63

Center Mats........... 65

Cards 69

© Evan-Moor Corp. • EMC 2870 • Take It to Your Seat Centers—Language Teacher Instructions 59

Name _____

Skill: Choose correct prepositions

I Know Prepositions

Circle the word that goes with each picture.

1.

in   out

2.

on   off

3.

to   from

4.

out   with

60 Written Practice

Take It to Your Seat Centers—Language • EMC 2870 • © Evan-Moor Corp.

Take It to Your Seat Centers

Prepositions

Skill: Show meaning of prepositions in sentences

Some words help tell **where** something is.

He is **in** bed.

1. Lay out the mats.
2. Lay out the cards.
3. Match the sentence cards with the pictures.
4. Do the written practice activity.

The ball is **in**.

The hen is **on**.

© Evan-Moor Corp. • EMC 2870 • Take It to Your Seat Centers—Language

Center Cover 61

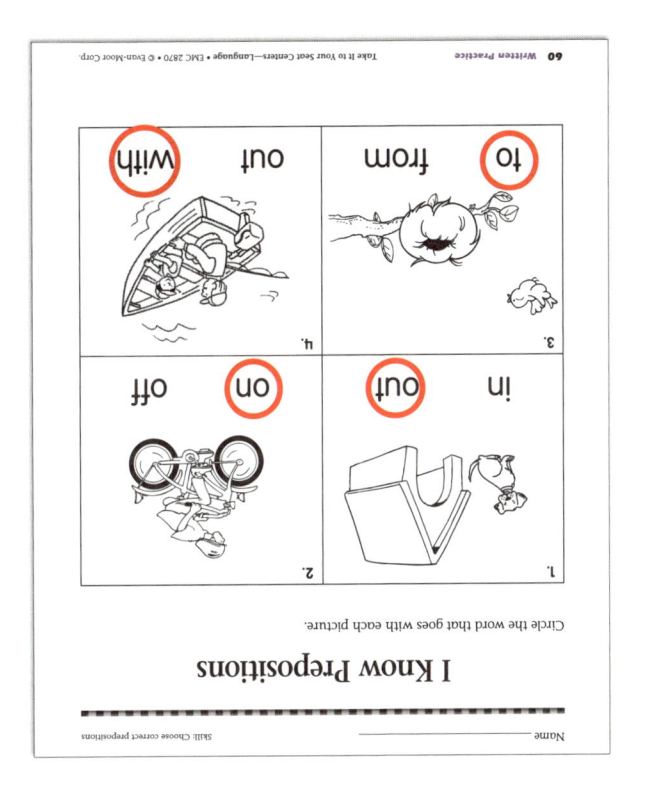

I Know Prepositions

Circle the word that goes with each picture.

1. **in** / (out)
2. (on) / off
3. (to) / from
4. out / (with)

Prepositions

Answer Key

Answer Key

Prepositions

Mat 1 — Prepositions

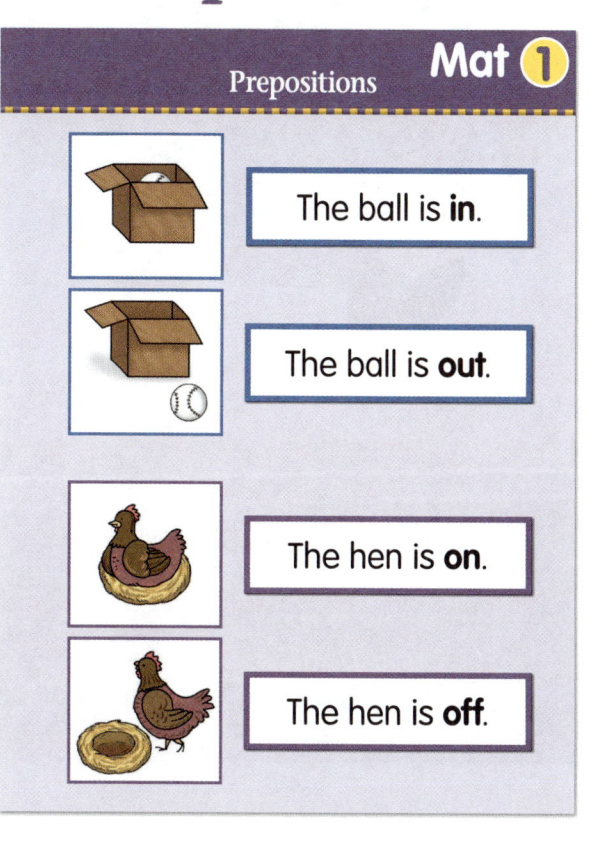

- The ball is **in**.
- The ball is **out**.
- The hen is **on**.
- The hen is **off**.

Mat 2 — Prepositions

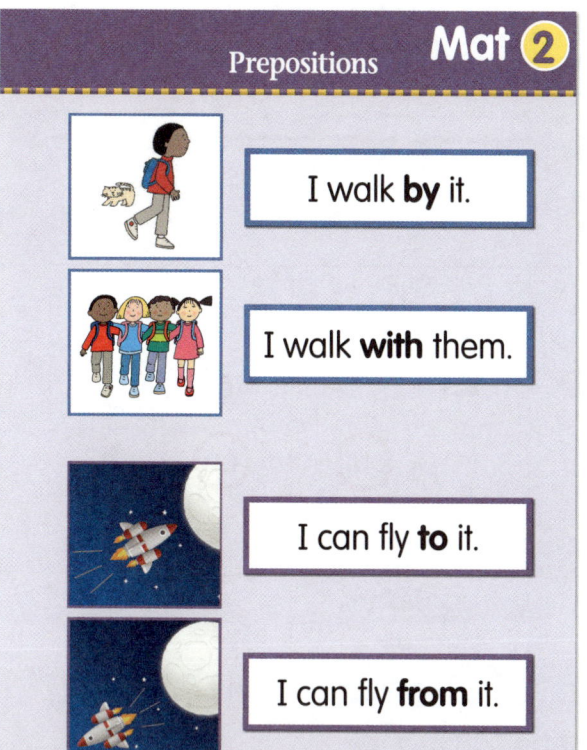

- I walk **by** it.
- I walk **with** them.
- I can fly **to** it.
- I can fly **from** it.

Mat 1

Prepositions

Center Mat

Take It to Your Seat Centers—Language • EMC 2870 • © Evan-Moor Corp.

Prepositions

Mat 2

Cards for Mats 1 and 2

The ball is **in**.

The ball is **out**.

The hen is **on**.

The hen is **off**.

I can fly **to** it.

I can fly **from** it.

I walk **by** it.

I walk **with** them.

Prepositions

EMC 2870
© Evan-Moor Corp.

Prepositions

EMC 2870
© Evan-Moor Corp.

Prepositions

EMC 2870
© Evan-Moor Corp.

Prepositions

EMC 2870
© Evan-Moor Corp.

Prepositions

EMC 2870
© Evan-Moor Corp.

Prepositions

EMC 2870
© Evan-Moor Corp.

Prepositions

EMC 2870
© Evan-Moor Corp.

Prepositions

EMC 2870
© Evan-Moor Corp.

Take It to Your Seat Centers

Capital Letters

Written Practice

Mats

Center Cover

Answer Key

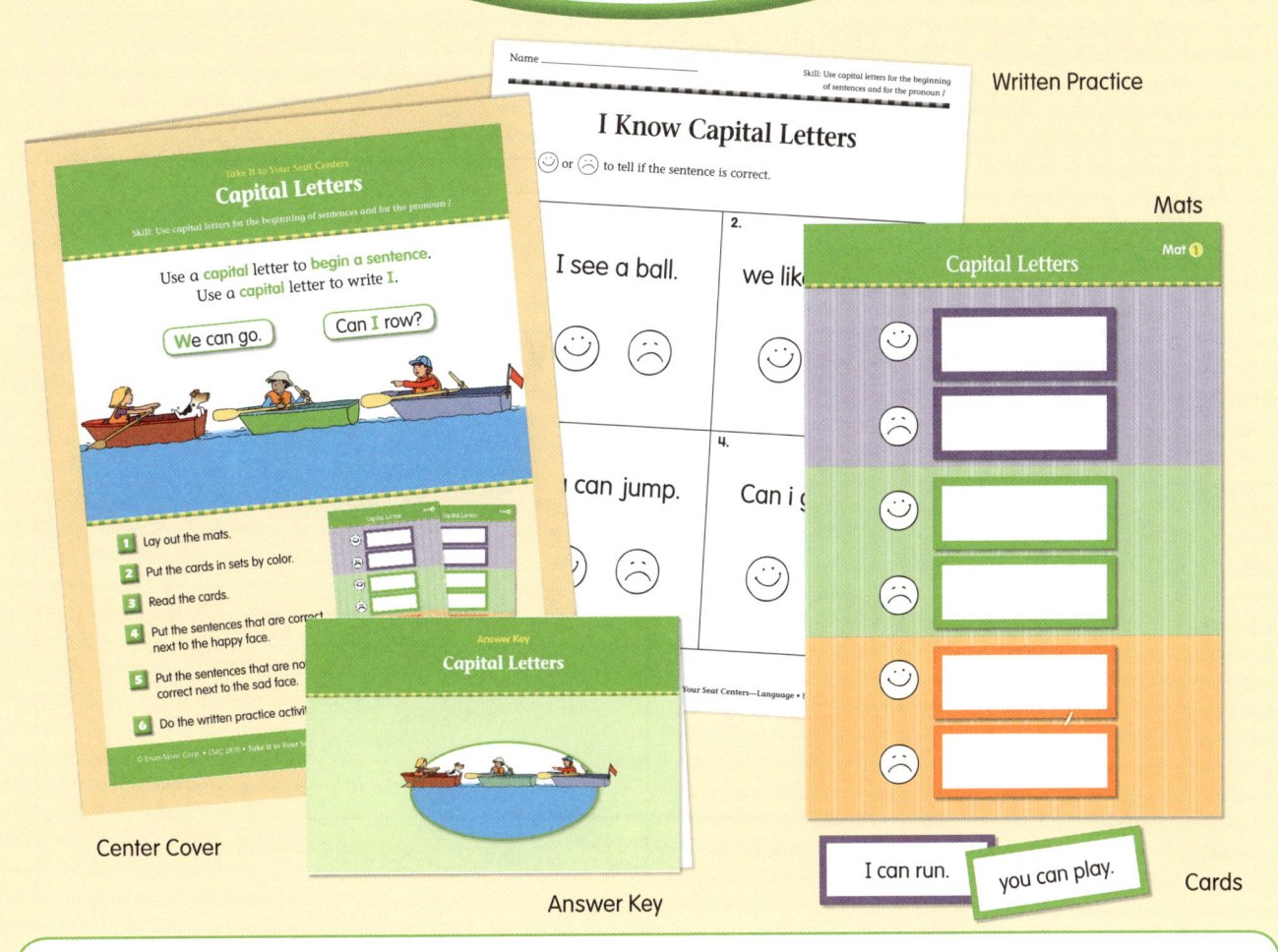

Cards

CCLS **K.2a** Capitalize the first word in a sentence and the pronoun *I*

Skill: Use capital letters for the beginning of sentences and for the pronoun *I*

Steps to Follow

1. **Prepare the center.** (See page 3.)
2. **Introduce the center.** State the goal. Say: *You will find sentences with the correct capital letters.*
3. **Teach the skill.** Demonstrate how to use the center.
4. **Practice the skill.** Have students complete the center tasks independently or with a partner.

Contents

Written Practice..... 72

Center Cover.......... 73

Answer Key............ 75

Center Mats........... 77

Cards 81

Teacher Instructions

Name _____

Skill: Use capital letters for the beginning of sentences and for the pronoun *I*

I Know Capital Letters

Color 🙂 or ☹ to tell if the sentence is correct.

1.

I see a ball.

🙂 ☹

2.

we like our cat.

🙂 ☹

3.

You can jump.

🙂 ☹

4.

Can i go too?

🙂 ☹

Take It to Your Seat Centers

Capital Letters

Skill: Use capital letters for the beginning of sentences and for the pronoun *I*

Use a **capital** letter to **begin a sentence**.
Use a **capital** letter to write **I**.

We can go.   Can I row?

1 Lay out the mats.

2 Put the cards in sets by color.

3 Read the cards.

4 Put the sentences that are correct next to the happy face.

5 Put the sentences that are not correct next to the sad face.

6 Do the written practice activity.

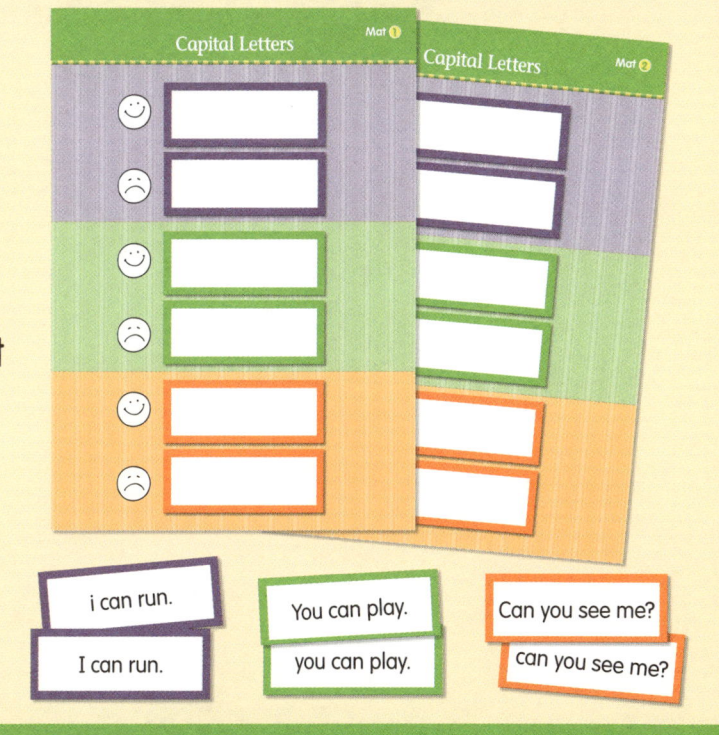

i can run.
I can run.

You can play.
you can play.

Can you see me?
can you see me?

Written Practice

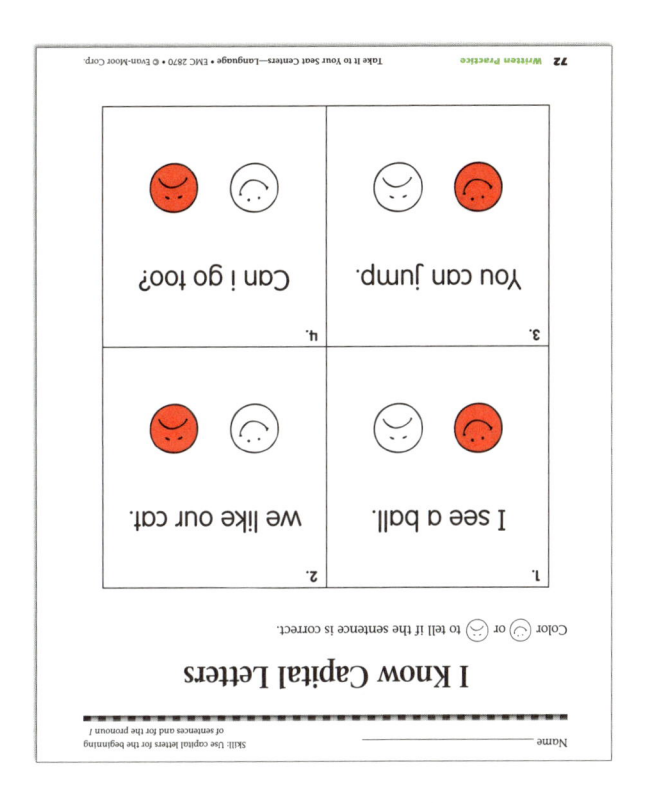

72 Written Practice

Name _____

I Know Capital Letters

Color 🙂 or 🙁 to tell if the sentence is correct.

1. I see a ball. 🙂 🔴
2. we like our cat. 🔴 🙂
3. You can jump. 🙂 🔴
4. Can i go too? 🔴 🙂

Skill: Use capital letters for the beginning of sentences and for the pronoun I

Take It to Your Seat Centers—Language • EMC 2870 • © Evan-Moor Corp.

(fold)

Answer Key

Capital Letters

Answer Key

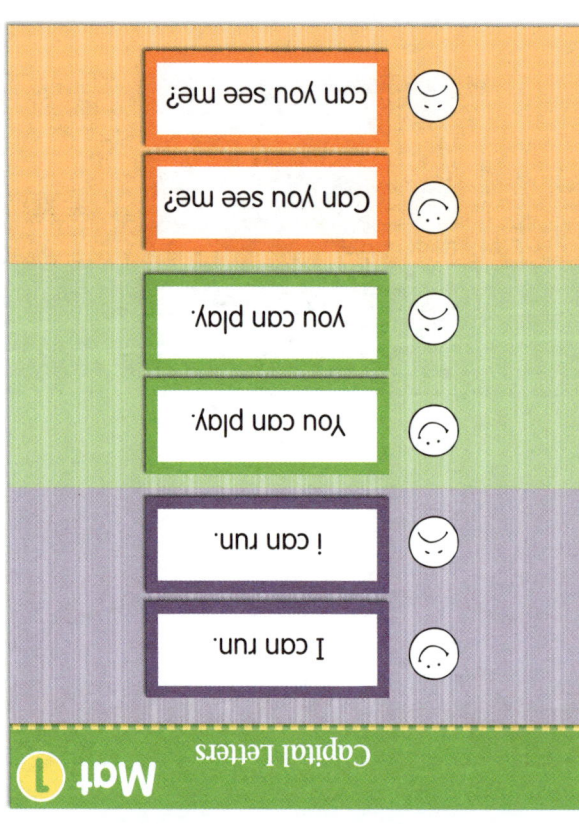

Capital Letters

Mat 1
Capital Letters

- ☺ I can run.
- ☹ i can run.
- ☺ You can play.
- ☹ you can play.
- ☺ Can you see me?
- ☹ can you see me?

Mat 2
Capital Letters

- ☺ What can I do?
- ☹ what can i do?
- ☺ Where can I go?
- ☹ where can i go?
- ☺ Look at my hat.
- ☹ look at my hat.

Capital Letters

Mat 1

Capital Letters

Mat 2

Cards for Mats 1 and 2

i can run.	I can run.
what can i do?	What can I do?
you can play.	You can play.
where can i go?	Where can I go?
can you see me?	Can you see me?
look at my hat.	Look at my hat.

Capital Letters **EMC 2870** • © Evan-Moor Corp.	**Capital Letters** **EMC 2870** • © Evan-Moor Corp.
Capital Letters **EMC 2870** • © Evan-Moor Corp.	**Capital Letters** **EMC 2870** • © Evan-Moor Corp.
Capital Letters **EMC 2870** • © Evan-Moor Corp.	**Capital Letters** **EMC 2870** • © Evan-Moor Corp.
Capital Letters **EMC 2870** • © Evan-Moor Corp.	**Capital Letters** **EMC 2870** • © Evan-Moor Corp.
Capital Letters **EMC 2870** • © Evan-Moor Corp.	**Capital Letters** **EMC 2870** • © Evan-Moor Corp.
Capital Letters **EMC 2870** • © Evan-Moor Corp.	**Capital Letters** **EMC 2870** • © Evan-Moor Corp.

Take It to Your Seat Centers

End Punctuation

Center Cover

Answer Key

Written Practice

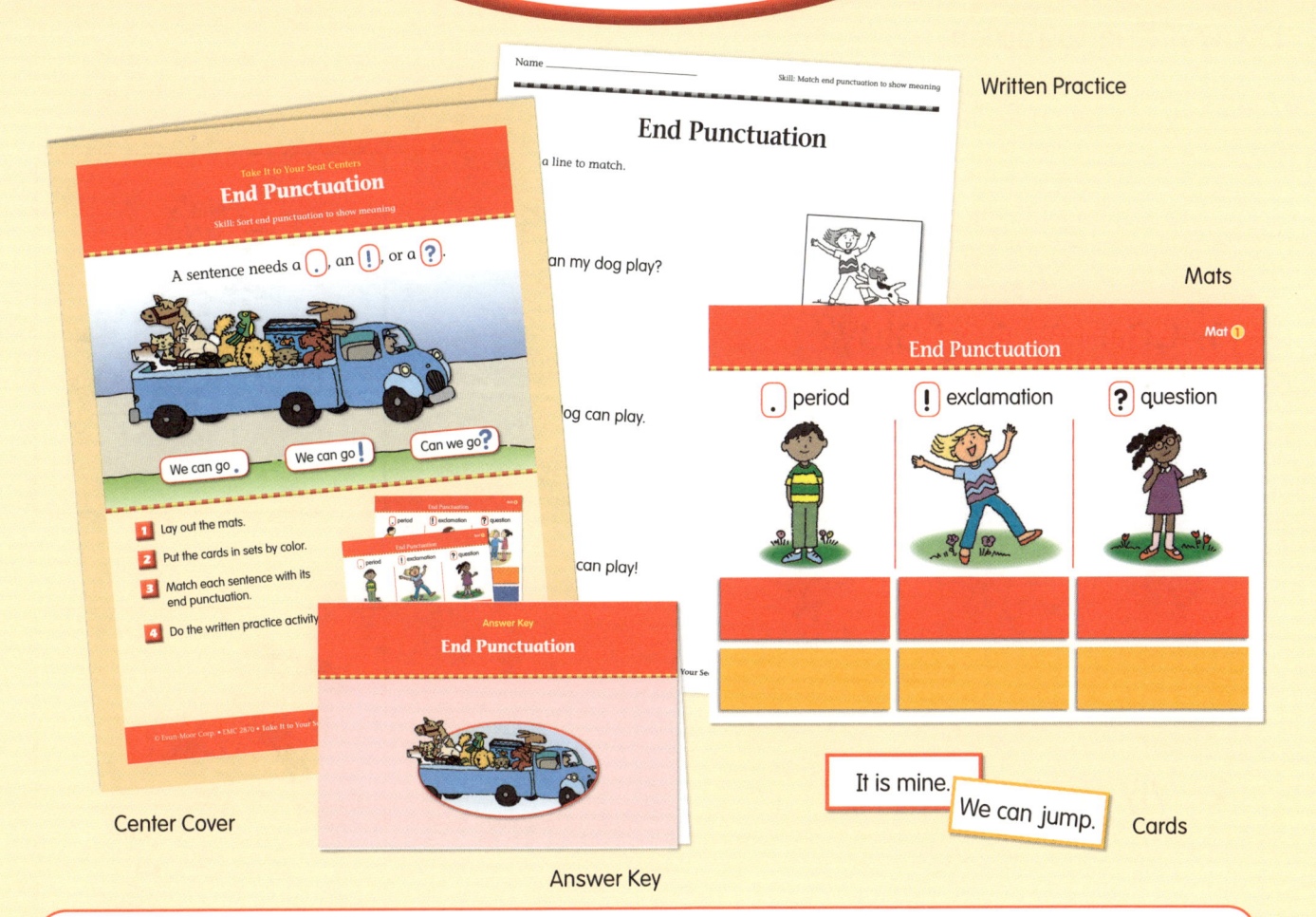

Mats

Cards

CCLS K.2b Recognize and name end punctuation

Skill: Sort and match end punctuation to show meaning

Steps to Follow

1. **Prepare the center.** (See page 3.)

2. **Introduce the center.** State the goal. Say: *You will sort sentences that end with periods, exclamation points, and question marks.*

3. **Teach the skill.** Demonstrate how to use the center.

4. **Practice the skill.** Have students complete the center tasks independently or with a partner.

Contents

Written Practice..... 84

Center Cover.......... 85

Answer Key............ 87

Center Mats 89

Cards 93

Name _____ Skill: Match end punctuation to show meaning

End Punctuation

Draw a line to match.

1. Can my dog play?

2. My dog can play.

3. My dog can play!

84 Written Practice   Take It to Your Seat Centers—Language • EMC 2870 • © Evan-Moor Corp.

Take It to Your Seat Centers

End Punctuation

Skill: Sort end punctuation to show meaning

A sentence needs a (.), an (!), or a (?).

We can go.   We can go!   Can we go?

1. Lay out the mats.
2. Put the cards in sets by color.
3. Match each sentence with its end punctuation.
4. Do the written practice activity.

It is mine.
We can jump.

© Evan-Moor Corp. • EMC 2870 • Take It to Your Seat Centers—Language   Center Cover   85

End Punctuation

Draw a line to match.

1. Can my dog play?
2. My dog can play.
3. My dog can play!

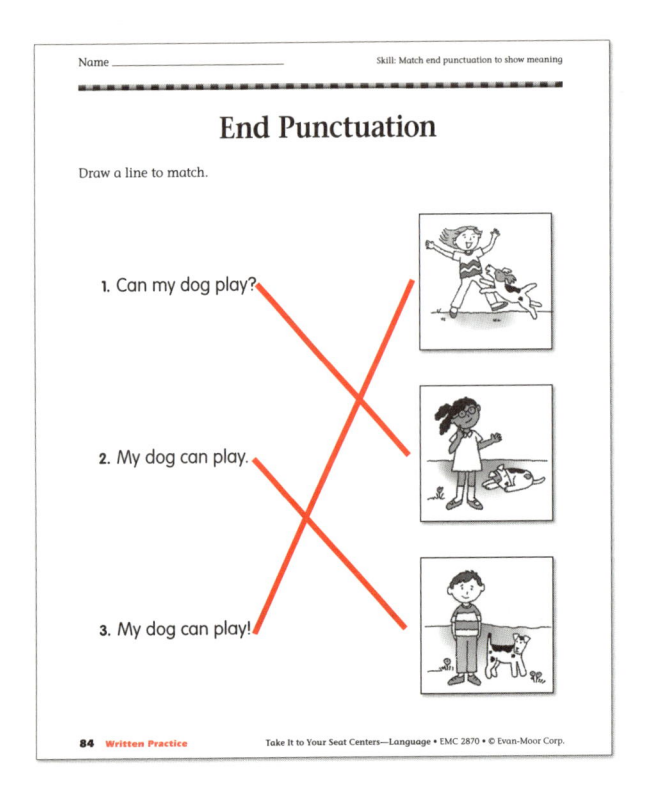

Written Practice

Answer Key

End Punctuation

Answer Key

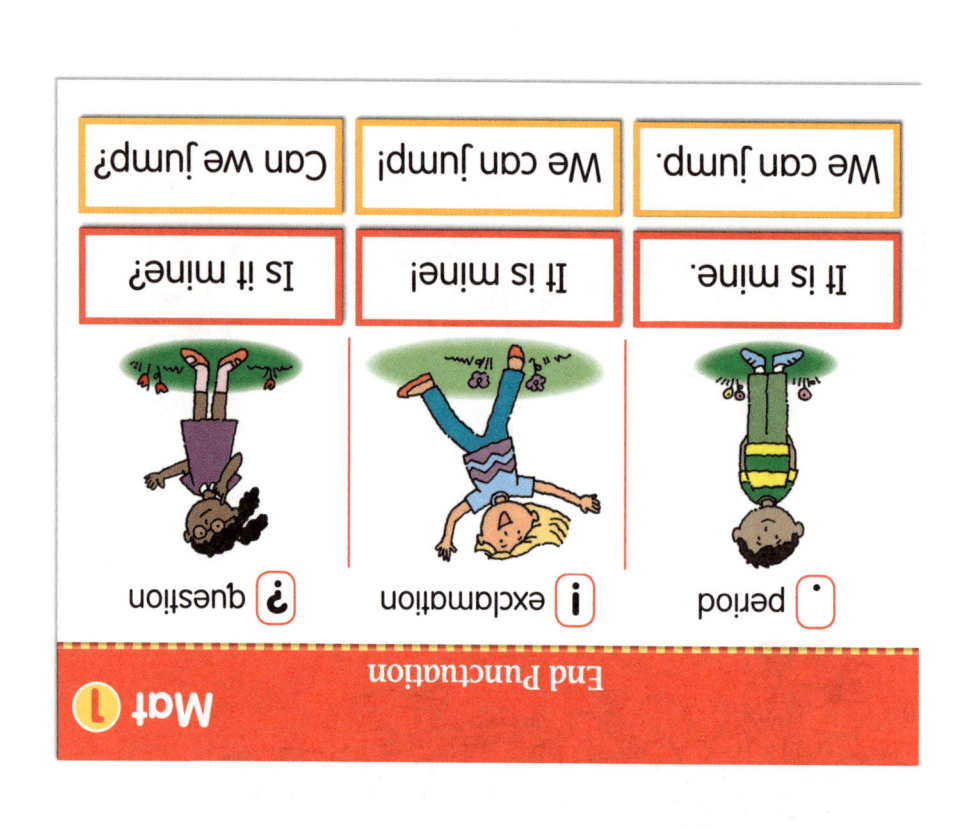

End Punctuation

Mat 1
End Punctuation

. period	! exclamation	? question
It is mine.	It is mine!	Is it mine?
We can jump.	We can jump!	Can we jump?

Mat 2
End Punctuation

. period	! exclamation	? question
She can run.	She can run!	Can she run?
We can play.	We can play!	Can we play?

Mat 1

End Punctuation

? question

! exclamation

. period

End Punctuation

Mat 2

? question

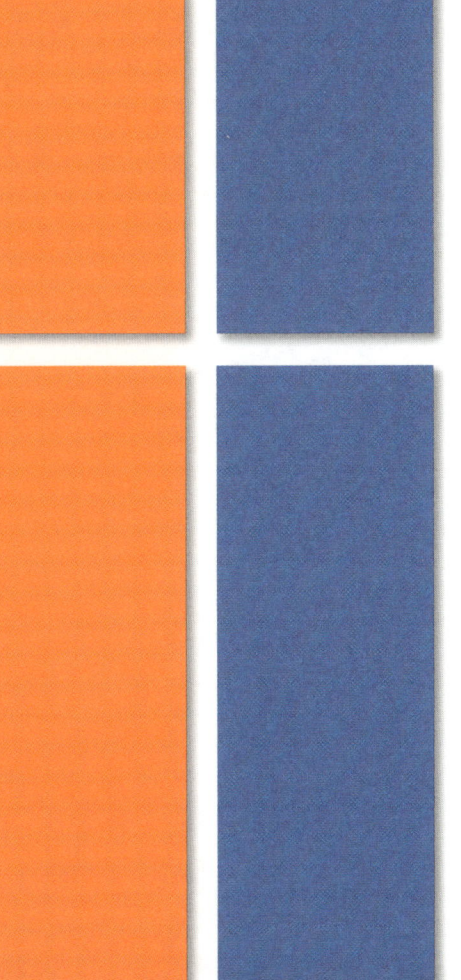

! exclamation

. period

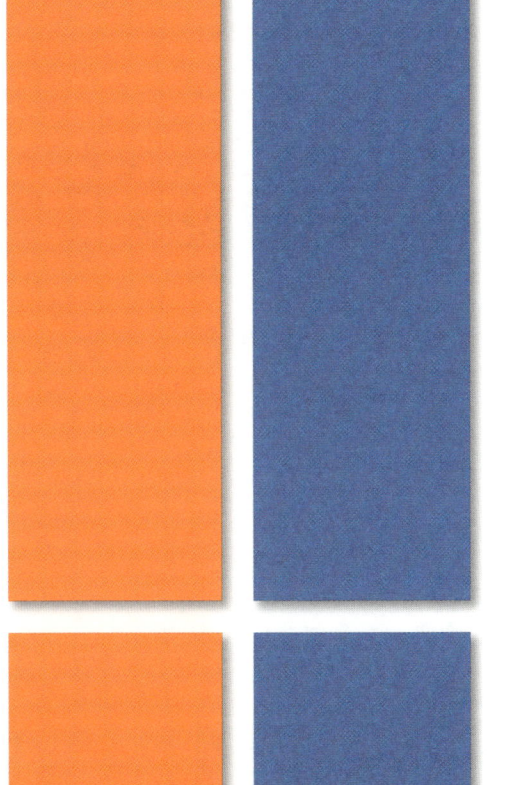

Cards for Mat 1

It is mine.	We can jump.
It is mine!	We can jump!
Is it mine?	Can we jump?

Cards for Mat 2

She can run.	We can play.
She can run!	We can play!
Can she run?	Can we play?

End Punctuation

EMC 2870 • © Evan-Moor Corp.

End Punctuation

EMC 2870 • © Evan-Moor Corp.

End Punctuation

EMC 2870 • © Evan-Moor Corp.

End Punctuation

EMC 2870 • © Evan-Moor Corp.

End Punctuation

EMC 2870 • © Evan-Moor Corp.

End Punctuation

EMC 2870 • © Evan-Moor Corp.

End Punctuation

EMC 2870 • © Evan-Moor Corp.

End Punctuation

EMC 2870 • © Evan-Moor Corp.

End Punctuation

EMC 2870 • © Evan-Moor Corp.

End Punctuation

EMC 2870 • © Evan-Moor Corp.

End Punctuation

EMC 2870 • © Evan-Moor Corp.

End Punctuation

EMC 2870 • © Evan-Moor Corp.

Take It to Your Seat Centers

Spell Words

Written Practice

Mats

Center Cover

Answer Key

Cards

CCLS **K.2c, K.2d** Write the letters for consonants and short-vowel sounds; spell simple words phonetically

Skill: Use letters and sounds to form words

Steps to Follow

1. **Prepare the center.** (See page 3.)
2. **Introduce the center.** State the goal. Say: *You will use letters and sounds to spell words.*
3. **Teach the skill.** Demonstrate how to use the center.
4. **Practice the skill.** Have students complete the center tasks independently or with a partner.

Contents

Written Practice..... 96

Center Cover.......... 97

Answer Key............ 99

Center Mats........... 101

Cards..................... 105

Name _____   Skill: Use letters and sounds to form words

I Can Spell Words

Look at the letters. Think about the sounds. Write the words.

| 1. __ t __ | 2. __ o __ | 3. __ i __ |
| 4. __ n __ | 5. __ w __ | 6. __ u __ |

96 Written Practice   Take It to Your Seat Centers—Language • EMC 2870 • © Evan-Moor Corp.

Take It to Your Seat Centers

Spell Words

Skill: Use letters and sounds to form words

Words are made up of **letters** and **sounds**.

1. Lay out the mats.
2. Lay out the cards.
3. Put the cards in the boxes to make words that match the pictures.
4. Do the written practice activity.

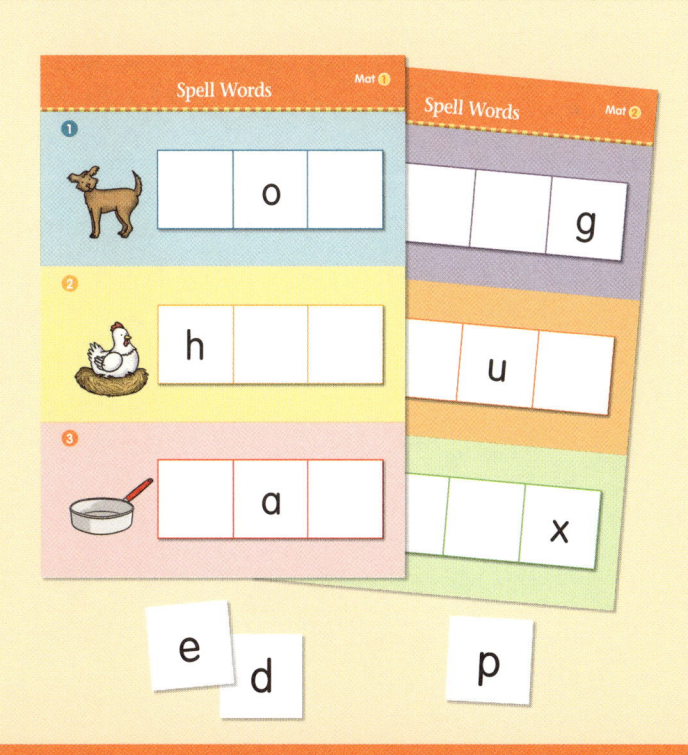

© Evan-Moor Corp. • EMC 2870 • Take It to Your Seat Centers—Language

Written Practice

I Can Spell Words

Look at the letters. Think about the sounds. Write the words.

1. hat
2. fox
3. six
4. ten
5. web
6. run

Skill: Use letters and sounds to form words

Spell Words

Answer Key

Answer Key
Spell Words

Mat 1
Spell Words

1. dog
2. hen
3. pan

Mat 2
Spell Words

1. dig
2. cup
3. box

Mat 1

Spell Words

1

| | o | |

2

| h | | |

3

| | a | |

Spell Words

Mat 2

1

		g

2

	u	

3

		x

Cards for Mat 1

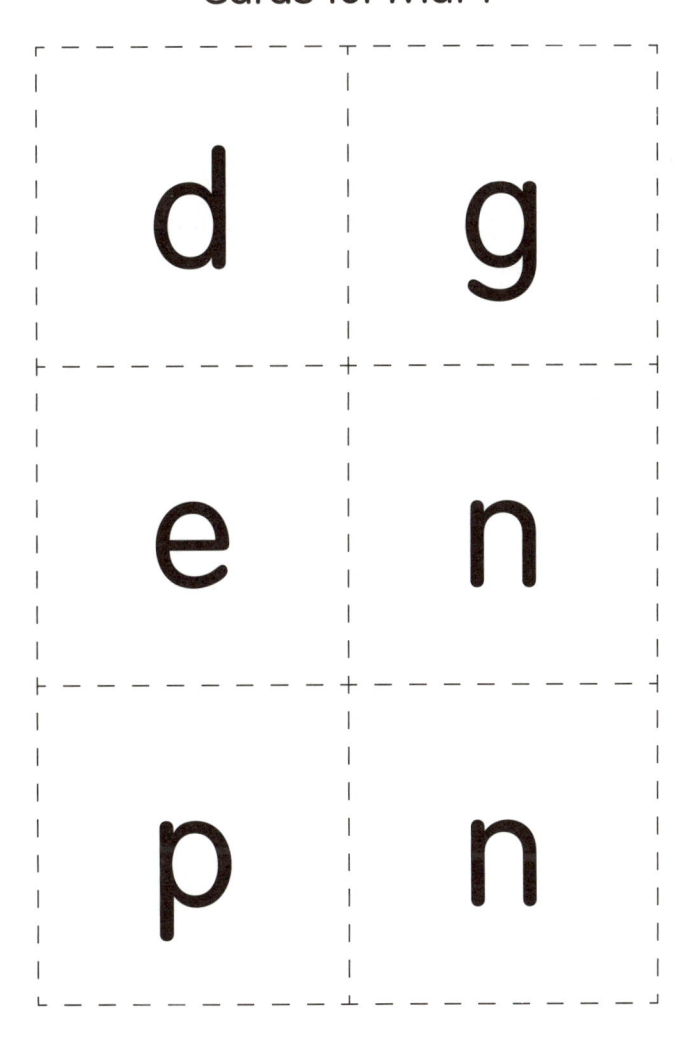

d	g
e	n
p	n

Cards 105

Spell Words

EMC 2870
© Evan-Moor Corp.

Spell Words

EMC 2870
© Evan-Moor Corp.

Spell Words

EMC 2870
© Evan-Moor Corp.

Spell Words

EMC 2870
© Evan-Moor Corp.

Spell Words

EMC 2870
© Evan-Moor Corp.

Spell Words

EMC 2870
© Evan-Moor Corp.

Cards for Mat 2

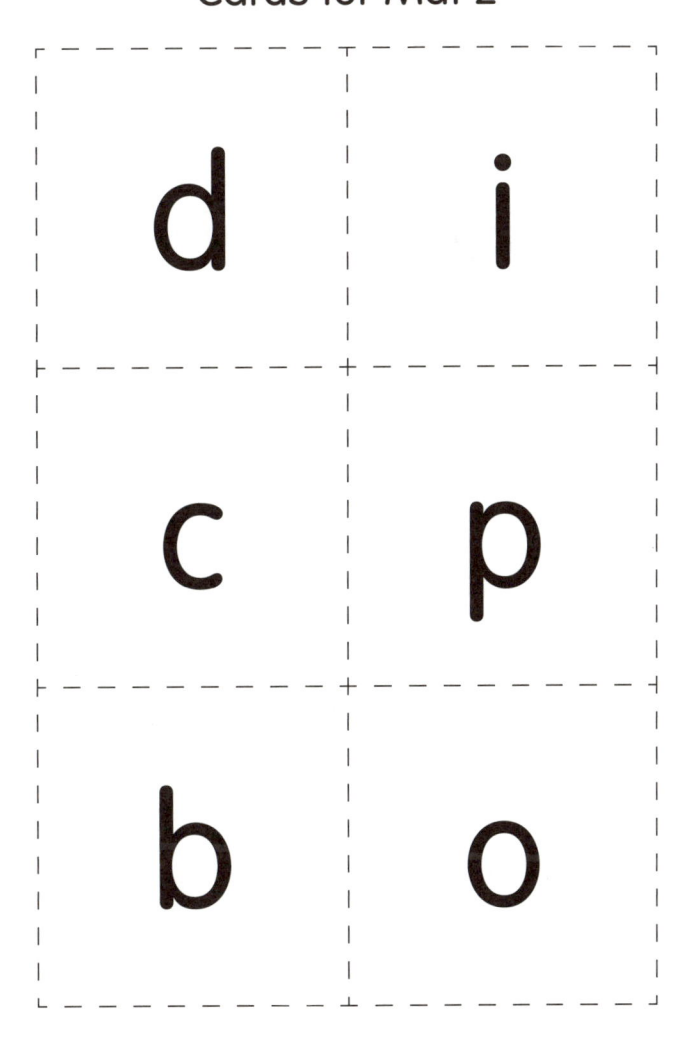

d	i
c	p
b	o

Spell Words	**Spell Words**
EMC 2870 © Evan-Moor Corp.	EMC 2870 © Evan-Moor Corp.
Spell Words	**Spell Words**
EMC 2870 © Evan-Moor Corp.	EMC 2870 © Evan-Moor Corp.
Spell Words	**Spell Words**
EMC 2870 © Evan-Moor Corp.	EMC 2870 © Evan-Moor Corp.

Take It to Your Seat Centers

Multiple-Meaning Words

Written Practice

Mats

Center Cover

Answer Key

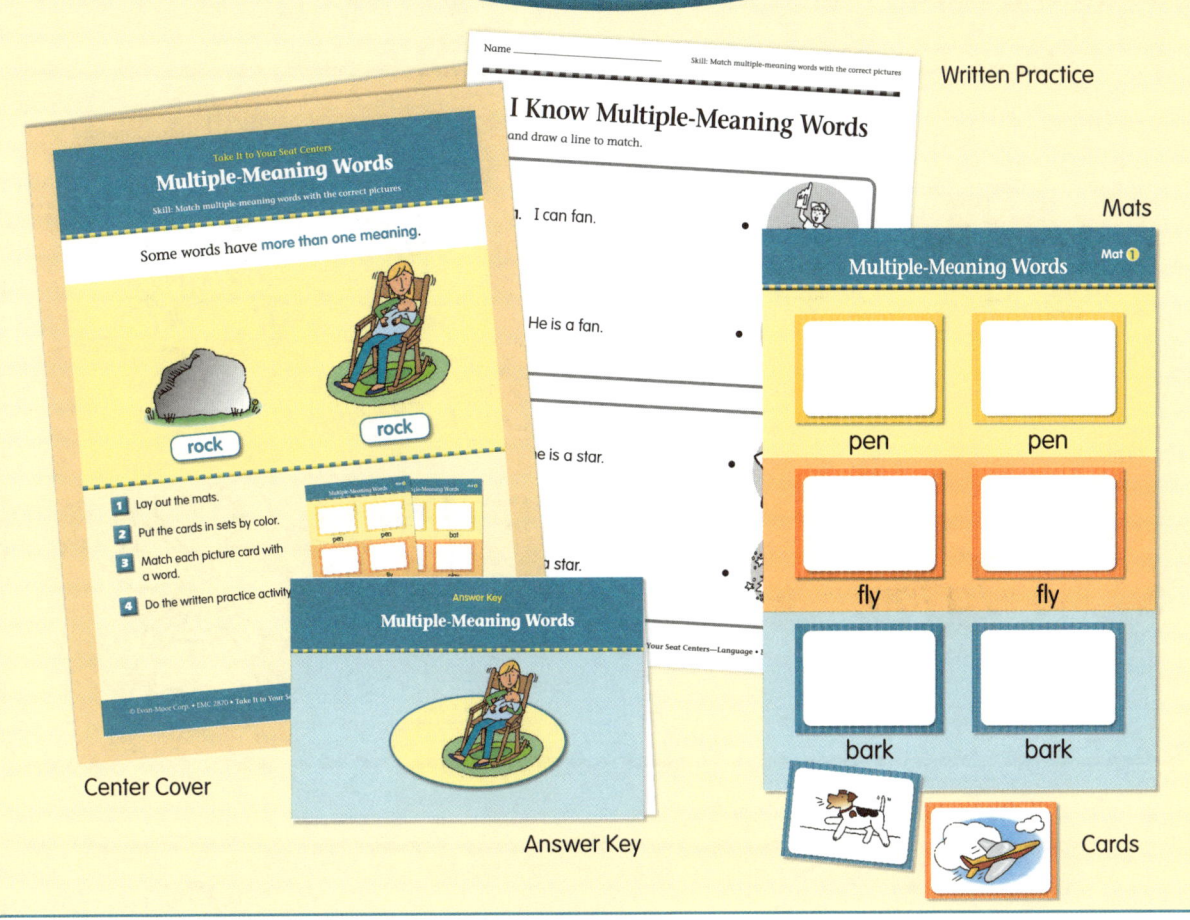

Cards

CCLS K.4 Determine or clarify the meaning of multiple-meaning words and phrases based on kindergarten reading and content

Skill: Match multiple-meaning words with the correct pictures

Steps to Follow

1. **Prepare the center.** (See page 3.)
2. **Introduce the center.** State the goal. Say: *You will match words that have more than one meaning to the correct pictures.*
3. **Teach the skill.** Demonstrate how to use the center.
4. **Practice the skill.** Have students complete the center tasks independently or with a partner.

Contents

Written Practice..... 110

Center Cover.......... 111

Answer Key............ 113

Center Mats........... 115

Cards..................... 119

I Know Multiple-Meaning Words

Read and draw a line to match.

1. I can fan.

2. He is a fan.

3. She is a star.

4. It is a star.

Take It to Your Seat Centers

Multiple-Meaning Words

Skill: Match multiple-meaning words with the correct pictures

Some words have more than one meaning.

rock

rock

1. Lay out the mats.
2. Put the cards in sets by color.
3. Match each picture card with a word.
4. Do the written practice activity.

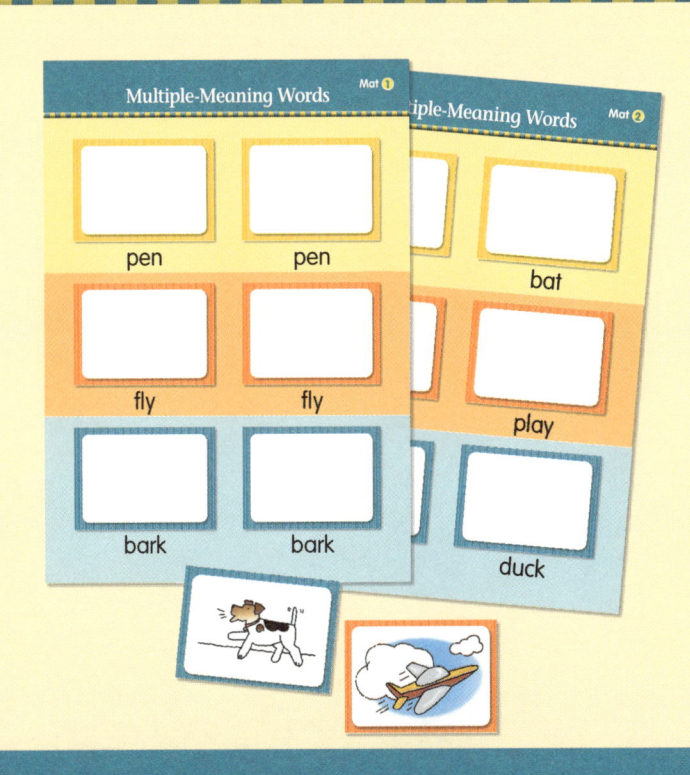

© Evan-Moor Corp. • EMC 2870 • Take It to Your Seat Centers—Language

Center Cover 111

Take It to Your Seat Centers—Language • EMC 2870 • © Evan-Moor Corp.

Written Practice

(fold)

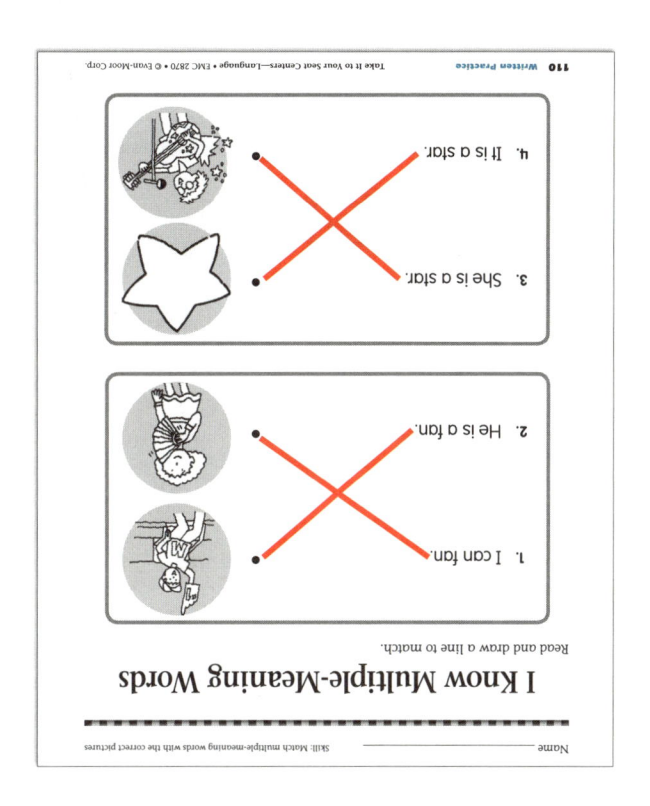

Name _____

Skill: Match multiple-meaning words with the correct pictures

I Know Multiple-Meaning Words

Read and draw a line to match.

1. I can fan.
2. He is a fan.

3. She is a star.
4. It is a star.

Written Practice • 110

Take It to Your Seat Centers—Language • EMC 2870 • © Evan-Moor Corp.

Answer Key

Multiple-Meaning Words

Answer Key

Multiple-Meaning Words

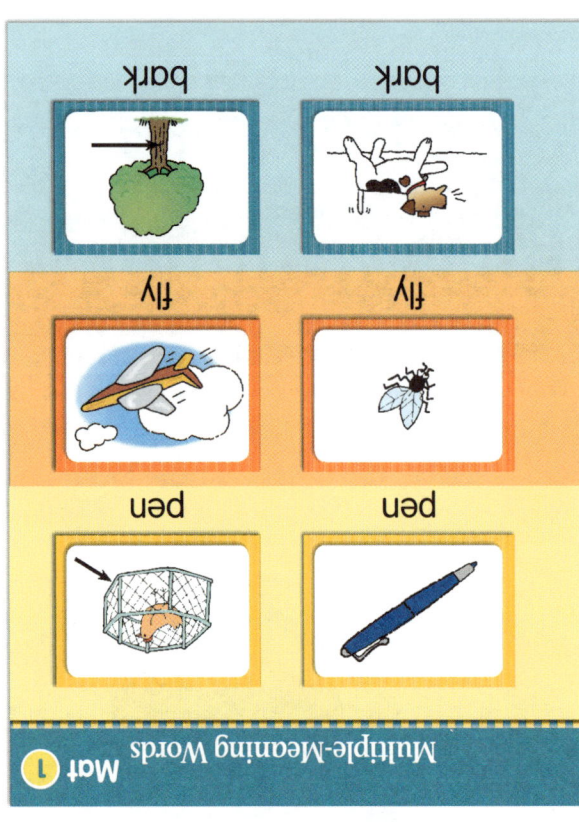

Mat 1

pen	pen
fly	fly
bark	bark

Mat 2

bat	bat
play	play
duck	duck

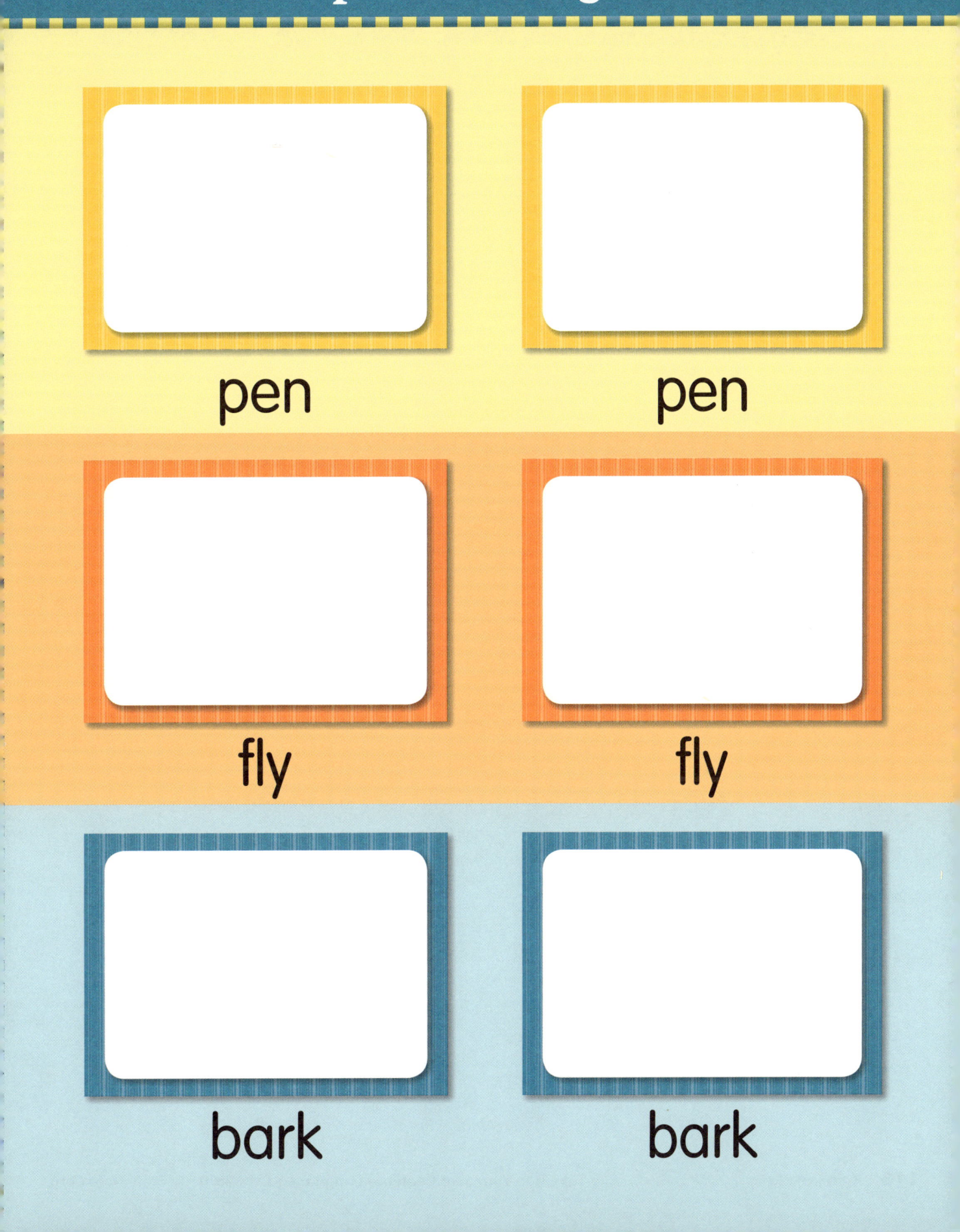

Multiple-Meaning Words

Mat 1

pen

pen

fly

fly

bark

bark

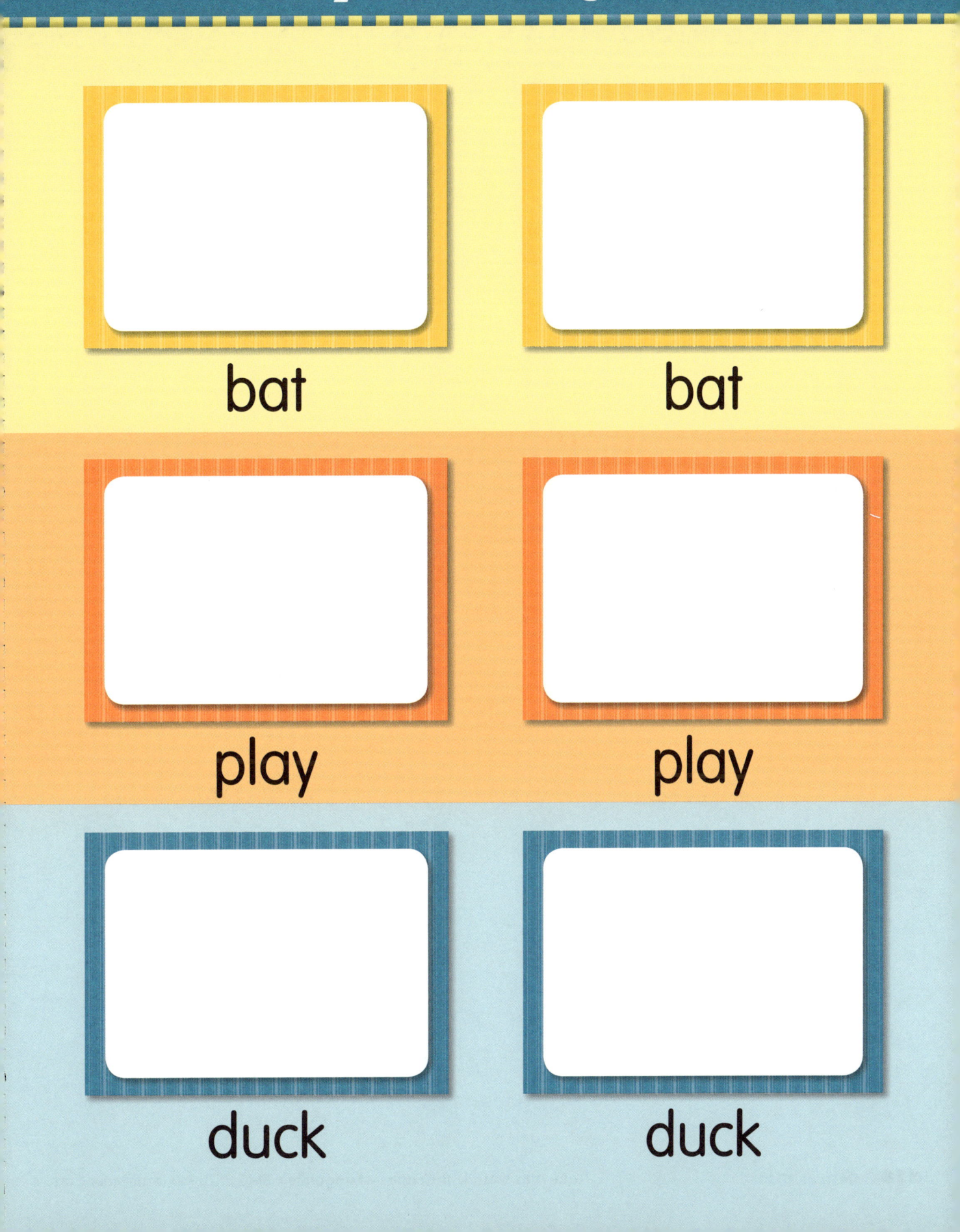

Multiple-Meaning Words

Mat 2

bat				bat

play			play

duck			duck

Cards for Mat 1

Multiple-Meaning Words

EMC 2870 • © Evan-Moor Corp.

Multiple-Meaning Words

EMC 2870 • © Evan-Moor Corp.

Multiple-Meaning Words

EMC 2870 • © Evan-Moor Corp.

Multiple-Meaning Words

EMC 2870 • © Evan-Moor Corp.

Multiple-Meaning Words

EMC 2870 • © Evan-Moor Corp.

Multiple-Meaning Words

EMC 2870 • © Evan-Moor Corp.

Cards for Mat 2

Multiple-Meaning Words

EMC 2870 • © Evan-Moor Corp.

Multiple-Meaning Words

EMC 2870 • © Evan-Moor Corp.

Multiple-Meaning Words

EMC 2870 • © Evan-Moor Corp.

Multiple-Meaning Words

EMC 2870 • © Evan-Moor Corp.

Multiple-Meaning Words

EMC 2870 • © Evan-Moor Corp.

Multiple-Meaning Words

EMC 2870 • © Evan-Moor Corp.

Take It to Your Seat Centers

Inflections and Affixes

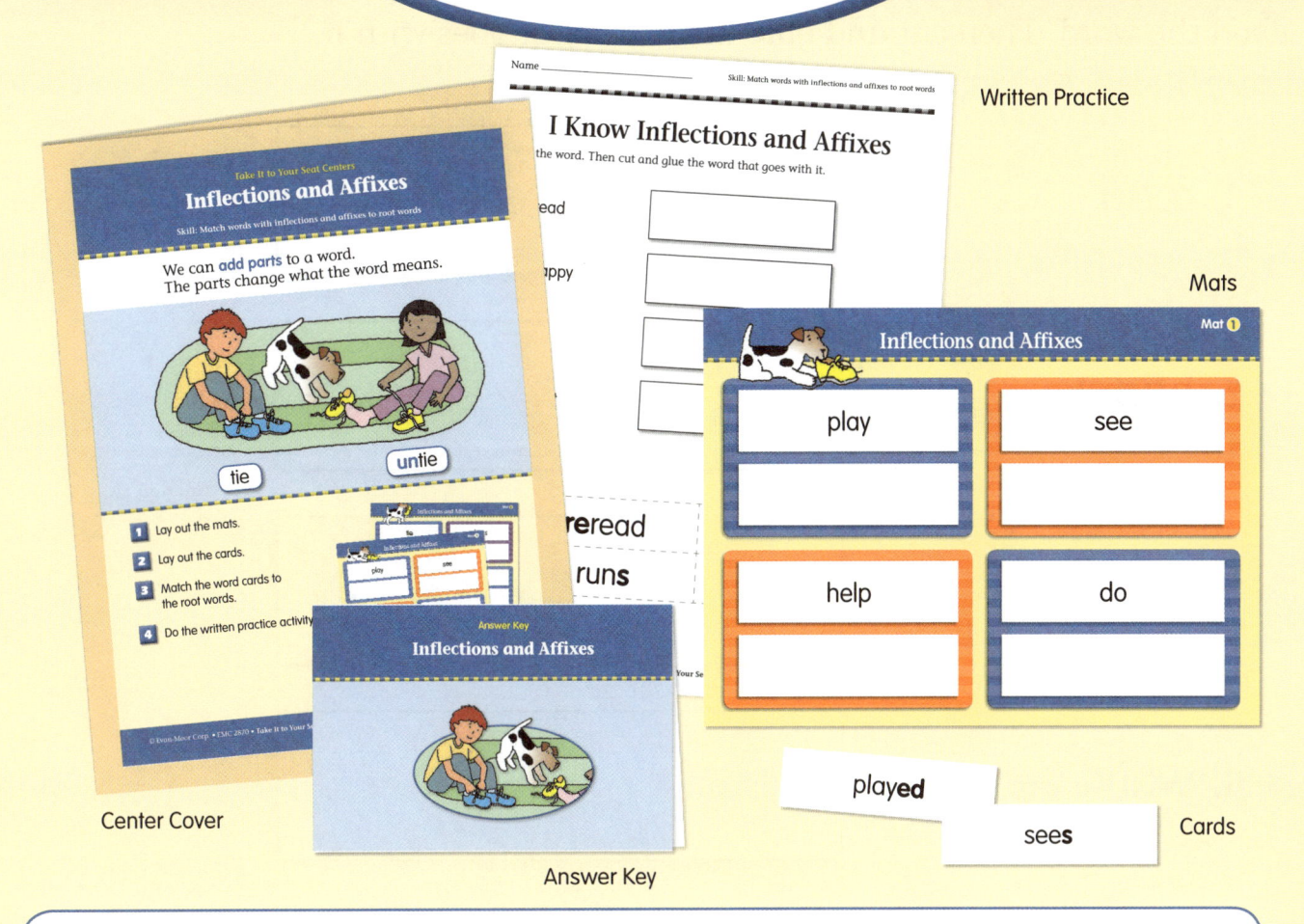

CCLS **K.4b** Use the most frequently occurring inflections and affixes as a clue to the meaning of an unknown word

Skill: Match words with inflections and affixes to root words

Steps to Follow

1. **Prepare the center.** (See page 3.)

2. **Introduce the center.** State the goal. Say: *You will match words with inflections and affixes to root words.*

3. **Teach the skill.** Demonstrate how to use the center.

4. **Practice the skill.** Have students complete the center tasks independently or with a partner.

Contents

Written Practice..... 124

Center Cover.......... 125

Answer Key............ 127

Center Mats........... 129

Cards..................... 133

© Evan-Moor Corp. • EMC 2870 • Take It to Your Seat Centers—Language

Teacher Instructions 123

Name _____

Skill: Match words with inflections and affixes to root words

I Know Inflections and Affixes

Read the word. Then cut and glue the word that goes with it.

1. read

2. happy

3. run

4. want

| **re**read | **un**happy |
| run**s** | want**ed** |

Take It to Your Seat Centers

Inflections and Affixes

Skill: Match words with inflections and affixes to root words

We can **add parts** to a word.
The parts change what the word means.

tie   untie

1. Lay out the mats.
2. Lay out the cards.
3. Match the word cards to the root words.
4. Do the written practice activity.

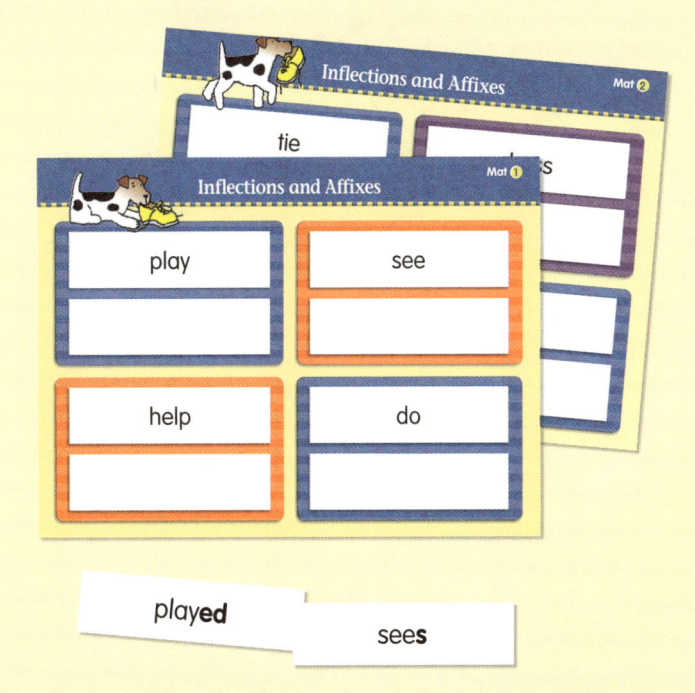

© Evan-Moor Corp. • EMC 2870 • Take It to Your Seat Centers—Language

Take It to Your Seat Centers—Language • EMC 2870 • © Evan-Moor Corp.

Written Practice

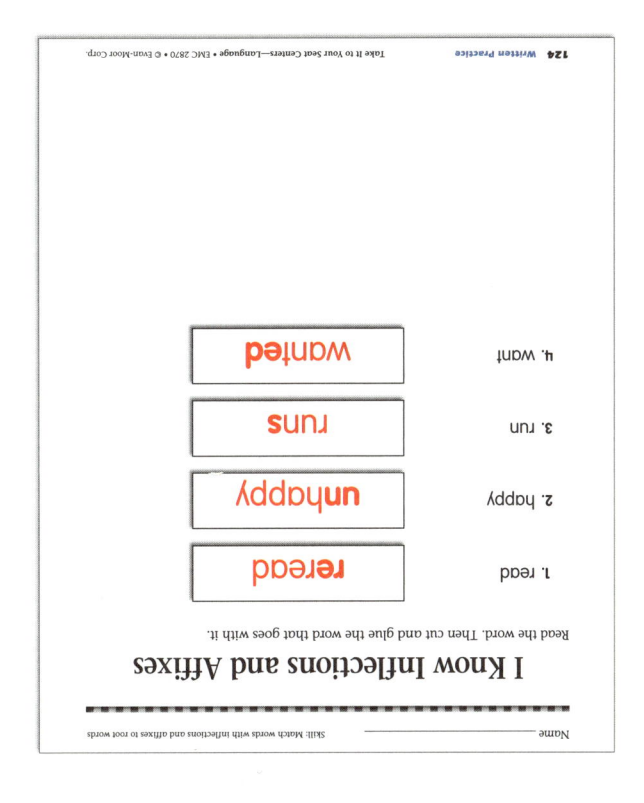

Name _____

Skill: Match words with inflections and affixes to root words

I Know Inflections and Affixes

Read the word. Then cut and glue the word that goes with it.

1. read — **reread**
2. happy — **unhappy**
3. run — **runs**
4. want — **wanted**

124 **Written Practice**

(fold)

Answer Key

Inflections and Affixes

Answer Key

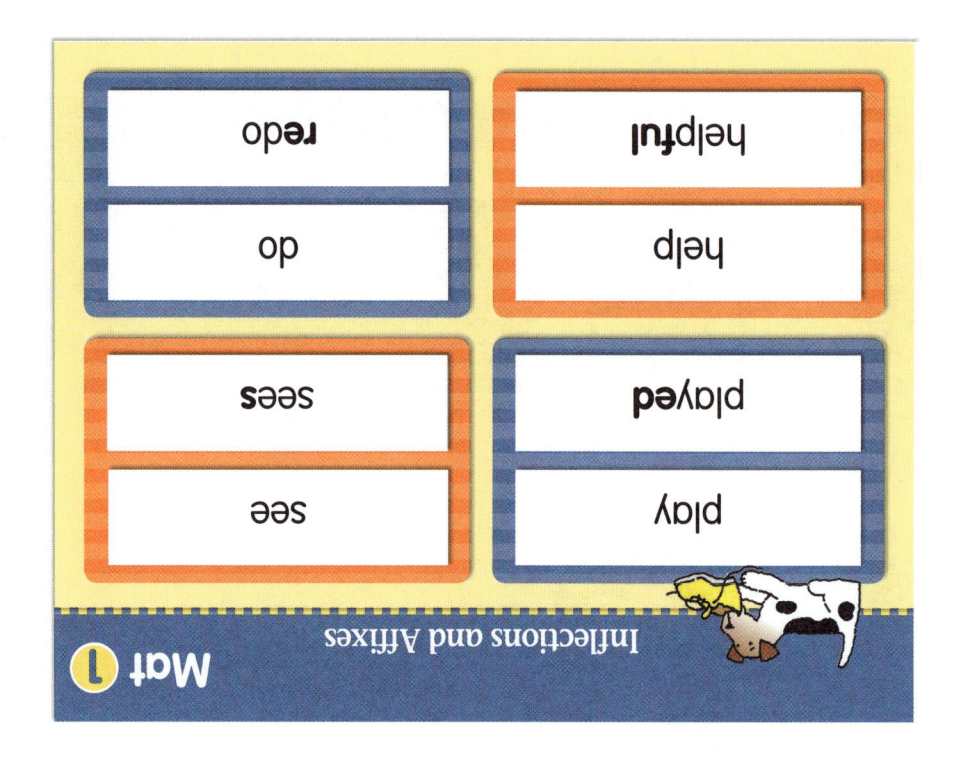

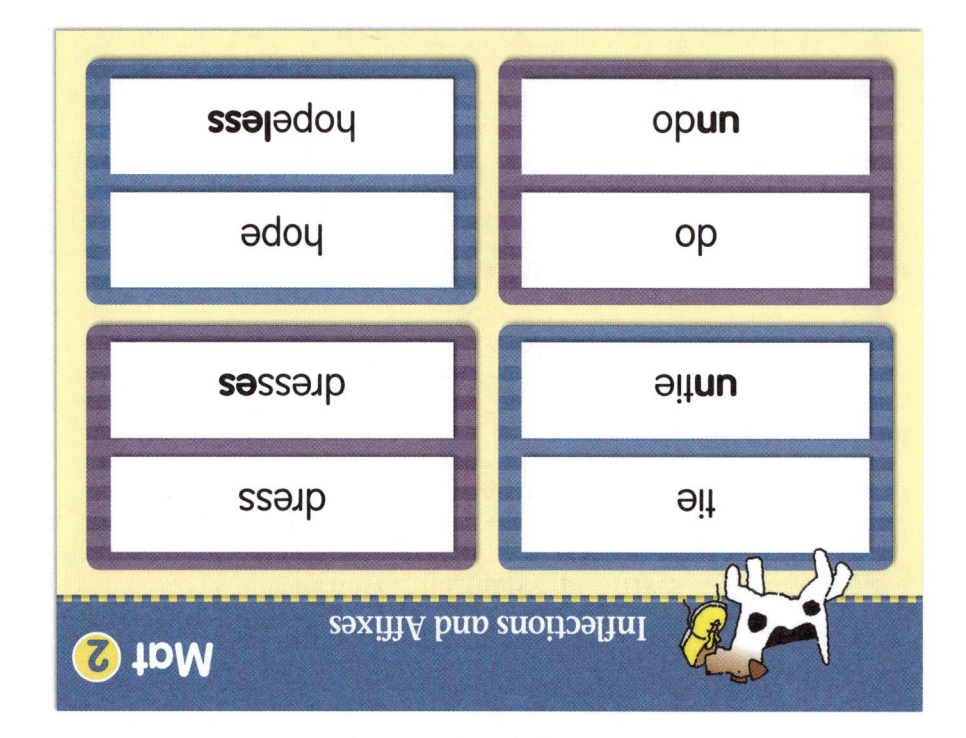

Inflections and Affixes

Mat 1

Inflections and Affixes

- play / played
- help / helpful
- see / sees
- do / redo

Mat 2

Inflections and Affixes

- tie / untie
- dress / dresses
- do / undo
- hope / hopeless

Inflections and Affixes

Mat 1

see

do

play

help

Inflections and Affixes

Mat 2

dress

hope

tie

do

Cards for Mat 1

play**ed**

redo

see**s**

help**ful**

Inflections and Affixes

EMC 2870 • © Evan-Moor Corp.

Inflections and Affixes

EMC 2870 • © Evan-Moor Corp.

Inflections and Affixes

EMC 2870 • © Evan-Moor Corp.

Inflections and Affixes

EMC 2870 • © Evan-Moor Corp.

Cards for Mat 2

untie

hope**less**

undo

dress**es**

Inflections and Affixes

EMC 2870 • © Evan-Moor Corp.

Inflections and Affixes

EMC 2870 • © Evan-Moor Corp.

Inflections and Affixes

EMC 2870 • © Evan-Moor Corp.

Inflections and Affixes

EMC 2870 • © Evan-Moor Corp.

Take It to Your Seat Centers

Sorting

Written Practice

Mats

Center Cover

Answer Key

Cards

CCLS **K.5a** Sort common objects into categories to gain a sense of the concepts the categories represent

Skill: Sort objects and name the groups

Steps to Follow

1. **Prepare the center.** (See page 3.)

2. **Introduce the center.** State the goal. Say: *You will sort items and name what kind of group they are in.*

3. **Teach the skill.** Demonstrate how to use the center.

4. **Practice the skill.** Have students complete the center tasks independently or with a partner.

Contents

Written Practice..... 138

Center Cover.......... 139

Answer Key............ 141

Center Mats 143

Cards 147

Name _____

Skill: Sort objects and name the groups

I Can Sort

Look at the groups. Cut and glue to sort.

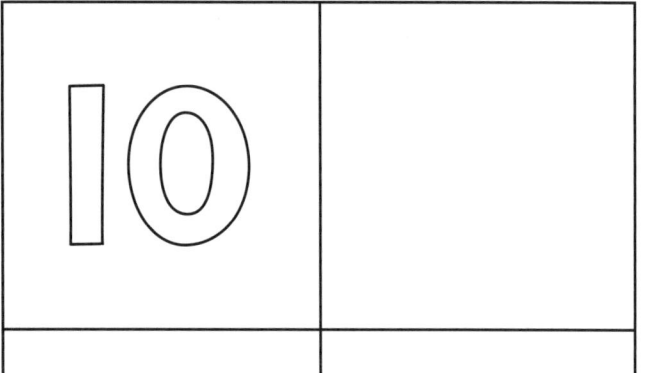

10	
	six

	(grass)
	(flower)

Numbers   five   2   one   7

Plants

138   Written Practice   Take It to Your Seat Centers—Language • EMC 2870 • © Evan-Moor Corp.

Take It to Your Seat Centers

Sorting

Skill: Sort objects and name the groups

Things can be sorted into **groups**.

hats

shoes

1. Lay out the mats.
2. Lay out the cards.
3. Sort the cards into groups on the mats.
4. Do the written practice activity.

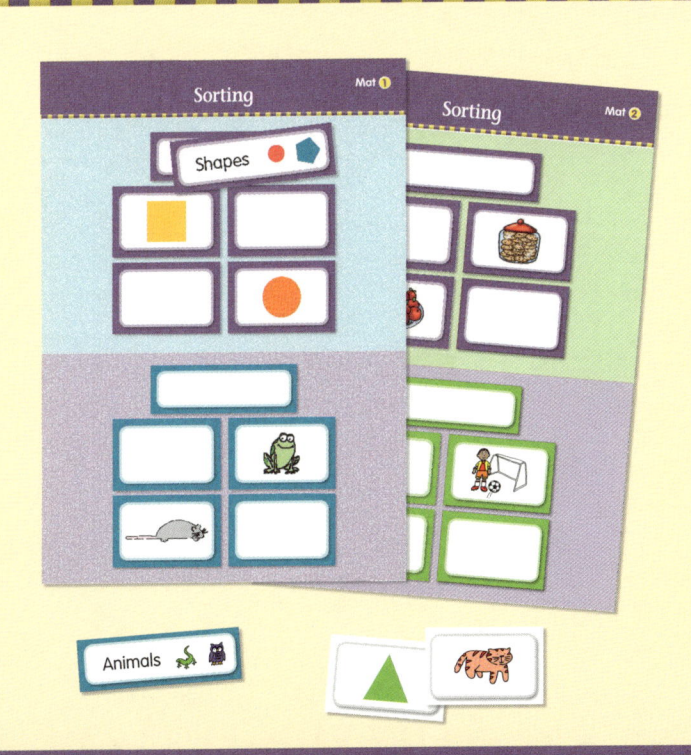

Take It to Your Seat Centers—Language • EMC 2870 • © Evan-Moor Corp.

Written Practice

(fold)

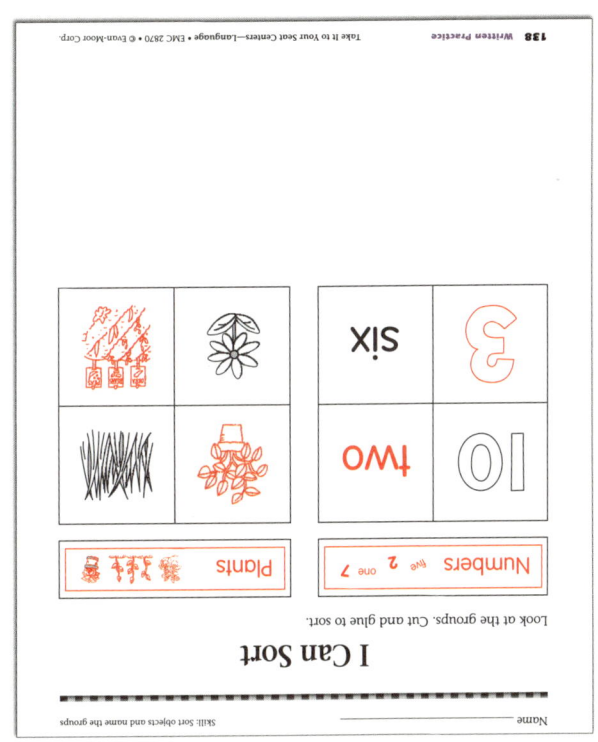

Answer Key

Sorting

Sorting

Answer Key

Mat 1

Sorting

Shapes

Animals

Mat 2

Sorting

Foods

Sports

Sorting

Mat 1

Sorting

Mat 2

Cards for Mats 1 and 2

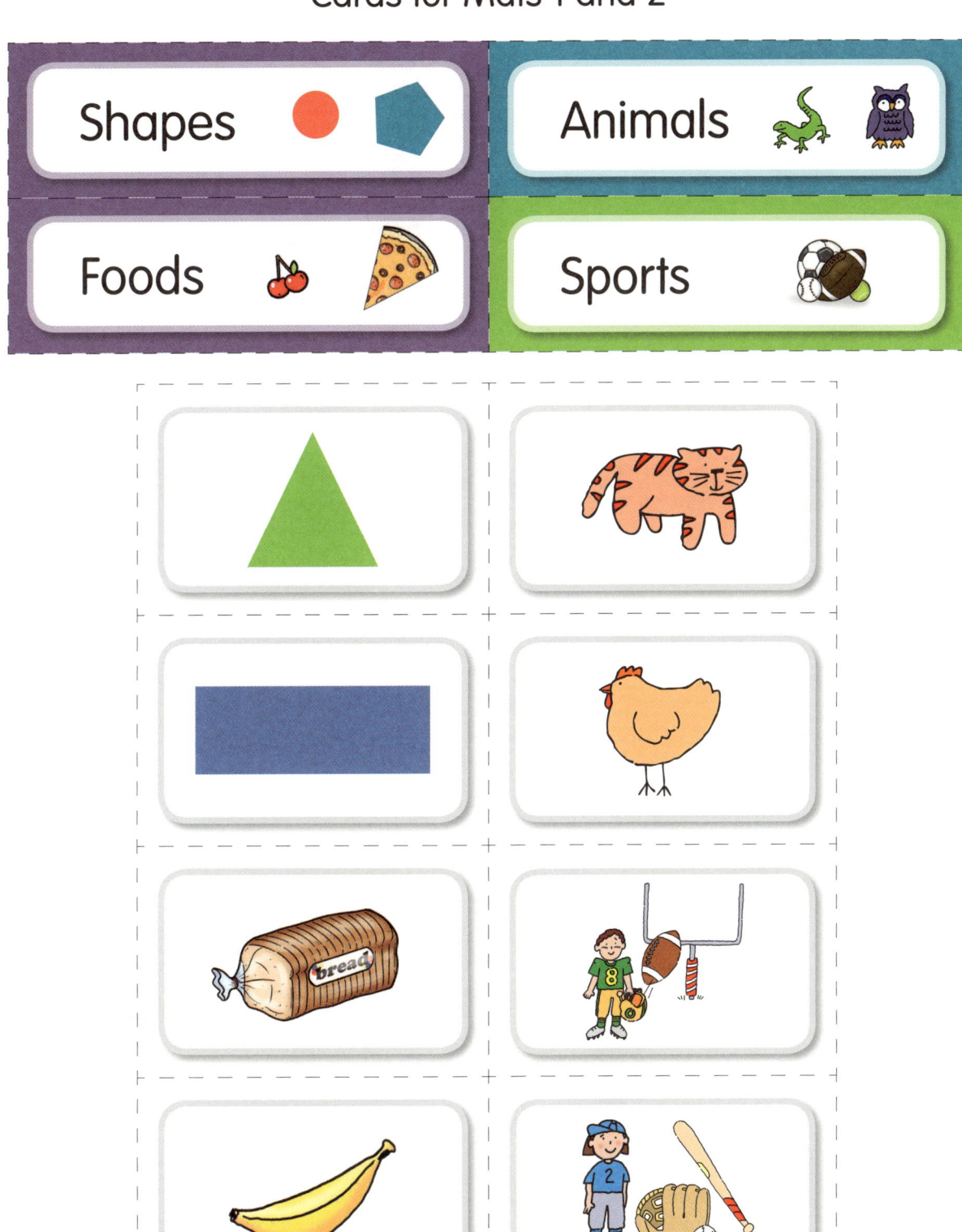

Shapes	Animals
Foods	Sports

Cards 147

Sorting
EMC 2870
© Evan-Moor Corp.

Sorting
EMC 2870
© Evan-Moor Corp.

Sorting
EMC 2870
© Evan-Moor Corp.

Sorting
EMC 2870
© Evan-Moor Corp.

Sorting
EMC 2870
© Evan-Moor Corp.

Sorting
EMC 2870
© Evan-Moor Corp.

Sorting
EMC 2870
© Evan-Moor Corp.

Sorting
EMC 2870
© Evan-Moor Corp.

Sorting
EMC 2870
© Evan-Moor Corp.

Sorting
EMC 2870
© Evan-Moor Corp.

Sorting
EMC 2870
© Evan-Moor Corp.

Sorting
EMC 2870
© Evan-Moor Corp.

Take It to Your Seat Centers

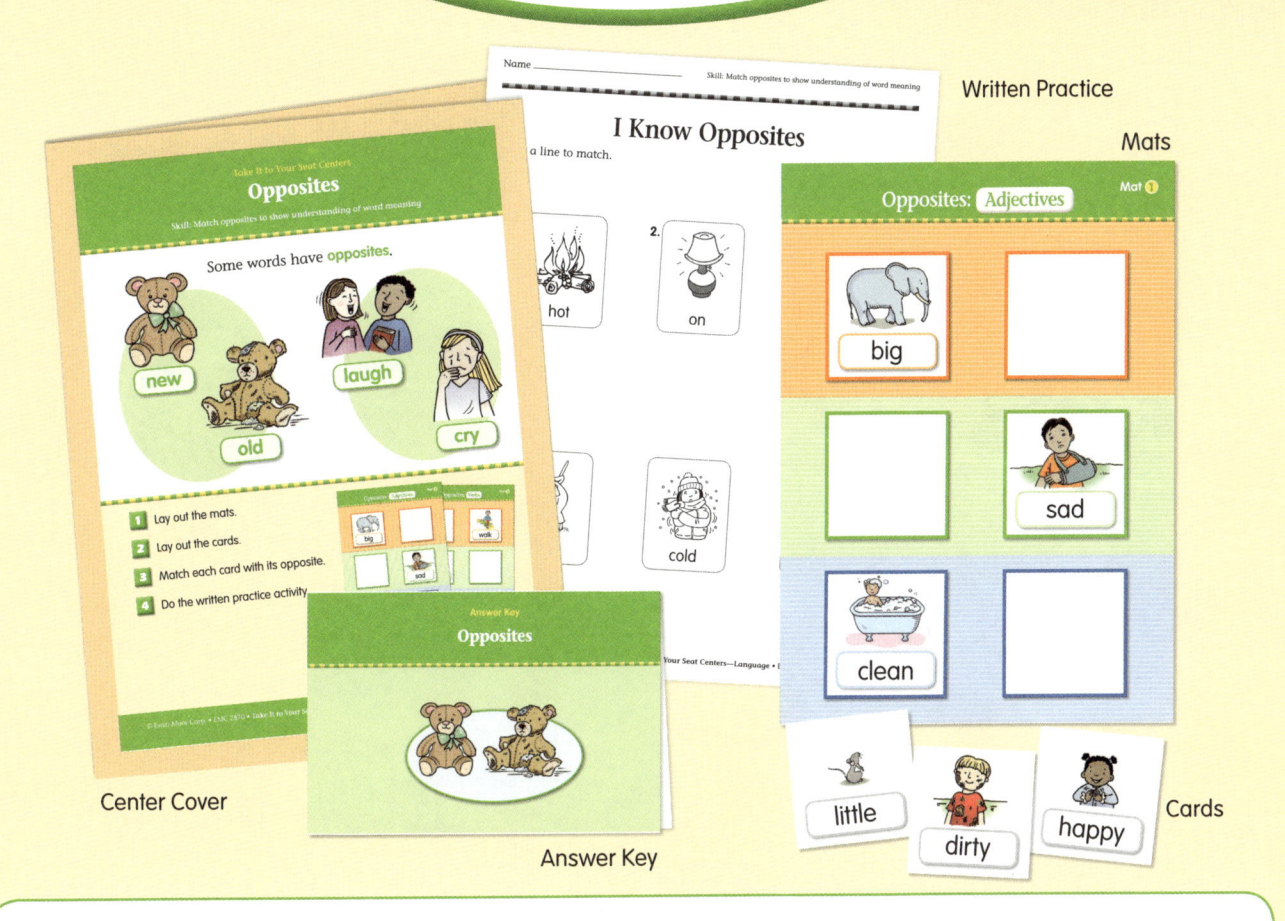

Opposites

Written Practice

Mats

Center Cover

Answer Key

Cards

CCLS **K.5b** Demonstrate understanding of frequently occurring verbs and adjectives by relating them to their opposites

Skill: Match opposites to show understanding of word meaning

Steps to Follow

1. **Prepare the center.** (See page 3.)

2. **Introduce the center.** State the goal. Say: *You will match words that are opposites.*

3. **Teach the skill.** Demonstrate how to use the center.

4. **Practice the skill.** Have students complete the center tasks independently or with a partner.

Contents

Written Practice..... 150

Center Cover.......... 151

Answer Key............ 153

Center Mats 155

Cards 159

Name _____   Skill: Match opposites to show understanding of word meaning

I Know Opposites

Draw a line to match.

1. hot

2. on

3. soft

hard

cold

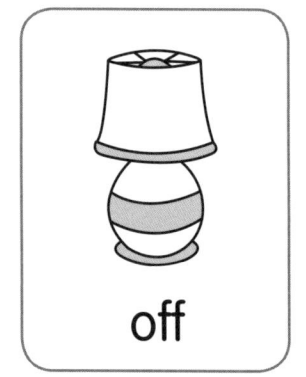

off

150 Written Practice   Take It to Your Seat Centers—Language • EMC 2870 • © Evan-Moor Corp.

Take It to Your Seat Centers

Opposites

Skill: Match opposites to show understanding of word meaning

Some words have **opposites**.

new

old

laugh

cry

1. Lay out the mats.
2. Lay out the cards.
3. Match each card with its opposite.
4. Do the written practice activity.

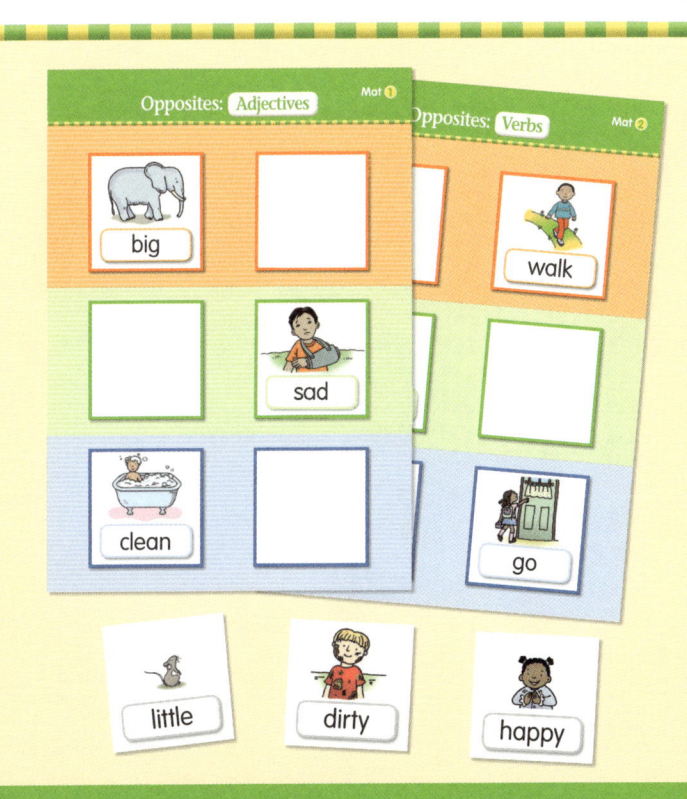

Opposites: Adjectives — Mat 1
big
sad
clean

Opposites: Verbs — Mat 2
walk
go

little   dirty   happy

© Evan-Moor Corp. • EMC 2870 • Take It to Your Seat Centers—Language

Name _____

I Know Opposites

Draw a line to match.

1. hot — soft
2. on — cold
3. soft — off

Written Practice

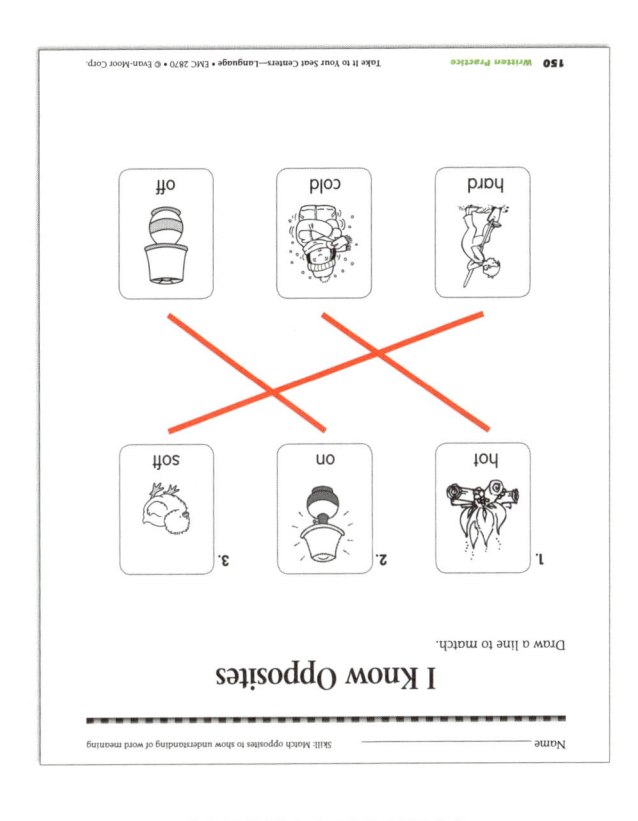

Answer Key

Opposites

Answer Key

Opposites

Mat 1 — Opposites: Adjectives

big	little
happy	sad
clean	dirty

Mat 2 — Opposites: Verbs

run	walk
stand	sit
come	go

Opposites: Adjectives

Mat 1

big

sad

clean

156 Center Mat Take It to Your Seat Centers—Language • EMC 2870 • © Evan-Moor Corp.

Opposites: Verbs

Mat 2

walk

stand

go

Cards for Mats 1 and 2

little	happy	dirty
run	sit	come

Opposites
EMC 2870
© Evan-Moor Corp.

Opposites
EMC 2870
© Evan-Moor Corp.

Opposites
EMC 2870
© Evan-Moor Corp.

Opposites
EMC 2870
© Evan-Moor Corp.

Opposites
EMC 2870
© Evan-Moor Corp.

Opposites
EMC 2870
© Evan-Moor Corp.